Dr. BBQ's
"Barbecue
All Year Long!"
Cookbook

50, 31, 15, 12, 81, 112, 124, 131, 170, 182, 201

Also by Ray Lampe

Dr. BBQ's Big-Time Barbecue Cookbook

Dr. BBQ's "Barbecue All Year Long!" Cookbook

RAY LAMPE

aka Dr. BBQ

St. Martin's Griffin ☙ New York

**This book is dedicated
to my mom and dad,
Lou and Ray Lampe**

www.stmartins.com

Book design by rlf design

Color photographs copyright © 2006 by Chris Vaccaro

Library of Congress Cataloging-in-Publication Data
Lampe, Ray.
    Dr. BBQ's "Barbecue all year long!" cookbook / Ray Lampe.—1st ed.
        p. cm.
    ISBN 0-312-34957-2
    EAN 978-0-312-34957-8
    1. Barbecue cookery.   I. Title.

TX840.B3L34 2006
641.5'784--dc22   2005054448

First Edition: May 2006
10 9 8 7 6 5 4 3 2 1

Contents

Foreword

In the introduction to Ray's first book, I predicted that it wouldn't be his only one, and it turns out that I was right. My only question after Ray told me about this book was how he would follow up a book where he revealed his innermost barbecue secrets. Well, as it turns out, Ray has quite a few more tricks up his barbecue apron, and he keeps on experimenting with recipes, technique, and presentation.

This book is about year-round barbecue with a vengeance. Ray has taken classic American holidays (and a few from other countries) and created menus for their celebration based on barbecue or grilling, and also included some sides and desserts that are not cooked outdoors but that fit the occasion. But the menus and recipes are just part of this book.

Barbecue guys are expected to be quite the characters, and Ray is a character's character. First, he didn't know he was a barbecuer and griller until he did it professionally. And he didn't know he was an author until he wrote a book. And he didn't know he was a barbecue celebrity until he saw his own photo in *Maxim*. And he didn't know that he was a historian—sort of—until he worked on this book and actually had to do some research. As Ray puts it, "The Internet is a wonderful thing." But Ray's history, like his 'cue, is not dry; rather, it is peppered with his own observations and opinions and sprinkled with witticisms. But where does he go from here? Look out for *The Lake Michigan Beach Diet* from Dr. BBQ if he keeps up this pace!

—Dave DeWitt

Acknowledgments

"Barbecue All Year Long!" has truly been a team effort. I get to be the guy who travels the country, cooking and having all the fun, but it couldn't happen without a long list of people. After my first book, we all agreed that we didn't want to do the same old barbecue book with a different cover for my second effort. So we were bouncing ideas around when my agent, Scott Mendell, came up with the idea of a barbecue lifestyle book. Obviously Scott is more than just a great agent; he's also part of the creative team. The lifestyle idea evolved into a series of reasons to barbecue, and ultimately a series of barbecue menus for events scheduled throughout the year.

The idea made this book great fun to write. I get wonderful inspiration from my friend Dave DeWitt, The Pope of Peppers. He loves to research interesting subjects, like why you should barbecue on the winter solstice, or the true reason to barbecue on Bastille Day.

Along with Scott and Dave, the team also includes the folks at St. Martin's Press, who have somehow turned a truck driver into an author. Michael Flamini deserves a huge amount of credit for everything I'll ever do in this business. He even stepped up to make the book look great by doing the food styling himself. Michael handpicked Chris Vaccaro to take the color photos at Michael's own farm.

Katherine Tiernan is way more than Michael's assistant. She has answered my questions and granted my wishes every single time I've needed it. Katherine has a very bright future.

Thank you to Matthew Shear, the St. Martin's Griffin publisher, as well as Amelie Littell, Cheryl Mamaril, James Sinclair, Ralph Fowler, and Edwin Tse, the top-notch production and design people.

Thank you to John Karle, from the St. Martin's publicity department, and his assistant, Shannon Twomey. They have put me in so many great places to promote myself and my books.

Thank you to all my cooking friends, known here as the Barbecue All Stars, who have given me great recipes to use. Thank you to all the other cooks who have crossed my path and inspired me.

Thank you to my good friends at Big Green Egg. I don't know what I'd do without the support of Jim Nufer, Lou West, and the rest of the gang in Atlanta.

Thank you to John Marcus and Chris Lilly, creators of *All-Star BBQ Showdown*. These guys put me on their TV show. The show also brought me together with Steve Murello, cameraman extraordinaire, who generously shared many of the pictures you see in this book.

A team effort indeed.

I Love Barbecue: An Introduction

I love barbecue. Have you heard? I love it when it's a noun, a verb, or an adjective. I love it spelled BBQ, Barbecue, Barbeque or Bar-B-Q. I love it cooked over wood, charcoal, pellets, gas, or even an electric heat source. So I see no reason to limit my barbecue activity to a few historically and politically correct occasions. And I absolutely refuse to limit my participation to the warm weather. So I wrote this book to celebrate year-round barbecue.

I think cooking outside for the Super Bowl is a great idea. I think New Year's Day is a great day to cook on the grill, and I think you should use the smoker for your Saint Paddy's Day corned beef. I wanted this book to be different than all the other barbecue books I have seen. Instead of doing it the way it's always been done, I wanted to look to the future, to a time when people will barbecue from January 1 until December 31. It's obvious to me that grills are growing wildly in popularity. Just look at all the places that sell them now. A few short years ago I had a hard time finding a kettle grill to buy for a

Christmas gift. Now there are whole stores devoted to selling grills all year, along with smokers, grilling tools, sauces, and rubs. As far as smokers go, the popularity of those, as well as of the many units that are proficient at grilling *and* smoking, is as hot as can be. People are really interested in this age-old art of real barbecue. I must thank the Food Network for a big helping hand with this. They now regularly cover the big barbecue events around the country, along with some great feature shows about the participants. You might even see me on some of them.

As long as we now have all of these nice new grills, let's start using them all year long. We follow the theme of cooking barbecue all year long in this book by creating menus for the many great opportunities throughout the year to have a barbecue celebration. Why not barbecue on some of the year's most beloved holidays like Christmas, Thanksgiving, and Easter? And how about celebrating some of the less well-known days of the year? Let's fire up the smoker for Patsy Cline's birthday.

"Sweet Dreams" is a good enough reason all by itself to have a party, but when you consider all of Patsy's great recordings, there's no way you can avoid celebrating the day. My friend Michael hates the heat and likes to celebrate the birthday of William Carrier, the father of air-conditioning. Well, that works for me and I put together a nice menu to keep cool on that day. During our research for these holidays, we realized that there was no National Barbecue Day. There is now, and it just so happens to fall on June 5, my birthday. Cinco de Mayo, Jack Daniel's birthday, and the summer solstice are also great days to fire up the cooker, so I've got menus for those days, too.

Now as much as I'd like you all to cook every menu and recipe in chronological order throughout the year, I also want you to keep your jobs, so feel free to mix and match and even to cook different recipes on different dates. As to the recipes, even I don't cook everything on the grill. Since it's a menu-oriented book, I needed to include many dessert and side dish recipes. I've got lots of those that come from the kitchen and go very well with the barbecue, as well as some that get the outdoor cooking treatment. I can tell you that this made it a lot of fun to write this book. The mixing and matching and the ability to think outside the barbecue box makes this a very special book. When I look at the list of recipes I think of the word "eclectic." When's the last time that the words "eclectic" and "barbecue" were used in the same sentence? Now, don't misunderstand that to mean nouveau barbecue, with a little pile of food served on a gigantic plate and topped with sea foam. The barbecue is

straightforward and often very traditional, but the combinations and the overall mix of recipes are definitely eclectic. As I combined my recipes into the menus, I realized that they didn't always serve the same amount of guests. I decided that it was okay that way, since adding a dish to a barbecue menu was common, and the main course is usually the star of the meal anyway.

A great way to get a feel for this book is to look at the beautiful color pictures taken by Chris Vaccaro on a small farm out in the country. I really like the way the photos portray the different ways barbecue can be presented. It's not just sticky ribs and grilled burgers anymore, though they're two of my favorites. Now you can serve barbecue on the china you inherited from your grandmother and pull out those fancy linen napkins Aunt Agnes gave you as a housewarming gift. There is the beautiful Easter Smokin' Leg of Lamb, sitting next to the Big Green Easter Egg. There's a photo of the Memorial Day Beefeater Martinis and Grilled Porterhouse Steaks that are a tribute to my dad, and a few things for Super Bowl Sunday that will make you want to put your feet up and grab the remote. I hope you enjoy those as much as I do.

My first book was a compilation of my life's experience. It was all in my head; we just had to turn it into a book. This book is different. It had to be created. Amazingly, I still had a few old barbecue circuit and family stories up my sleeve. It was great fun to weave them with the fun stuff my research provided, and at the same time with all the great recipes. I've also continued the fun tradition of getting recipes from Barbecue All Stars. This time we even have a couple of international barbecuers on that list: Ted Reader, aka King of the Q from Canada, and Jackie and Rick Weight, aka the Mad Cow team from Britain. Did I mention the drink recipes? There are plenty of those, too. Some are very traditional, and a couple are exciting new ones. There's even one called The Happy Doctor. It's a classic with a new name.

I hope you will get the fever to cook on your grill all year long. It's a passion I've had for many years, no matter where I lived. It's something I really enjoy, and with the help of my book, I hope you will enjoy it, too.

Dr. BBQ

Winter

▼▼▼▼▼▼▼▼▼▼▼▼▼▼▼

A Wonderful Time for Barbecue

Winter Solstice and Saturnalia:
A "Pagan" Celebration

Christmas:
Holiday Gift Grilling

New Year's Eve:
The Ultimate Revelry

New Year's Day:
Traditions

Groundhog Day:
Fair and Bright

Groundhog Day:
Clouds and Rain

Super Bowl Barbecue:
A Super 'Cue Party

Carnival:
Party-Time Outdoor Cooking

Valentine's Day:
The Romantic Grill

The Daytona 500:
Race Day Barbecue

▼▼▼▼▼

You might think it's weird that I would start a seasonal barbecue book with the end of the year, but I think of winter as a beginning and a new challenge for the barbecuer. Yes, it's true that I now live in Florida, and you're thinking, "How hard can it be to cook outdoors in January when the temperature's 65 degrees?" True, but it's also true that I used to live in Chicago, so I do have some experience with outdoor cooking in challenging conditions. I have personally cooked for a tailgate party in the parking lot at Soldier Field when the temperature was below zero. We had to use can koozies to keep our beers from freezing. Besides, recent surveys indicate that two-thirds of grill owners cook year-round, and you don't want to be on the short list, so layer up and get outside.

Keep the Cook Warm

The first priority is no frostbite for the cook. It's not that hard. Just use some sensible winter ideas. Try to cook during the warmest part of the day, midafternoon. Put a hook for your jacket and a rug for your boots by the door that you use to go out to the grill. Wear your long underwear and warm socks, and turn the heat down a little in the house so you'll also be comfortable when you're inside. Spend as little time outdoors as possible. If you position your cooker so you can see the temperature from the inside, you won't have to go outside much at all. I like to grill indirectly or cook low and slow, so that I don't have to spend too much time watching over the food. If you're really wimpy, you can get one of those heaters that mount right on the twenty-pound propane bottle. They work very well. Just don't light your pants on fire.

The Right Equipment

Obviously, cold air will suck the heat right out of your grill or smoker. But if you use a well-insulated cooker, like the Big Green Egg with its thick ceramic walls, it will be able to hold the heat in without using an extreme amount of fuel. If you don't have a well-insulated cooker, or don't want to buy one, you can use a fireproof welding blanket, available at welding supply stores, and place it over your grill when the lid is shut. This will insulate the grill and help prevent heat loss. Don't cover all the vents though, or you'll have no fire at all. It's also good to shield the grill from the wind as much as you can. Put it behind a fence, a wall, or even some bushes. Some of you more rural barbecue enthusiasts could also use the broken-down cars in your yard or your chicken coop to break the wind.

The Right Food

The winter barbecuer should avoid cooking things that will burn quickly. If you are going to grill, make it something quick like steaks or burgers. You don't want to have to babysit grilled chicken pieces with a sugary rub that could scorch during a short trip into the house. Instead, cook them indirectly. I like to cook whole chickens, game hens, roasts, and hams during the winter, as you can go out into the cold every half hour or so to check the food and fuel. Or grill foods that take a very short amount of time, like the Stuffed White Mushrooms in the winter solstice menu. It's a good idea to cook a full grill in the winter, too. You can freeze some for a later "bonus" barbecue from the microwave, but what I really like to do is cook a few other things that will join a different recipe at a later date. If I'm cooking a chicken for dinner, I'll also cook a roll of sausage to be used later in the Smoked Sausage, Leek, and Potato Soup, or some catfish for the Smoked Catfish Spread. By the way, the sausage freezes well; the catfish does not, but it will easily hold for a couple days in the refrigerator.

Cooking Times

The cold will affect the total cooking time for food from the grill, particularly if it's combined with a howling wind, but once you get your cooker up to temp and the food on, it shouldn't be an issue. Allow a little extra time (and fuel) for getting the cooker ready. After the startup, keep the temperature up and the lid closed. Letting in a batch of subzero air will wreak havoc on your temp, and of course your time. Last but certainly not least, use a heated platter to transfer the food to the house. You can set the platter on top of a warm oven, or just run it under hot water for a few minutes and then dry it off. Try to cover the food with a lid or aluminum foil as quickly as possible, too.

If you keep all these things in mind, cooking barbecue all year shouldn't be any problem at all. There are even some advantages to cooking during the winter. When the temperature is just right you can leave your beer outside or just use snow in your cooler. Think of all the money you'll save on ice! You'll probably see less of your freeloading neighbors, too. Odds are they won't be outside to smell the great food, so they won't be able to troll for an invite. Fewer people for a barbecue dinner means you have to cook less food, and that equals spending less money. Barbecuing in the winter could actually get you to an earlier retirement. So there you have it: no reason not to barbecue during the winter no matter where you are. Your friends and family will be glad you did.

Winter Solstice and Saturnalia: A "Pagan" Celebration

▼▼

The winter solstice, usually December 22, is the shortest day of the year. It was called "Yule" in the days before Christianity, and that word came from the Anglo-Saxon "yula" or "wheel" of the year. The ancient "pagan" ritual called for the Yule log to be fired up on the eve of the solstice and burned for twelve hours. These days, charcoal, wood, or even propane will be our Yule log. Actually, the ancient Romans were celebrating the rebirth of the sun and a renewal of growth. It is just downright weird that this "new growth" is the official start of winter and longer days. Go figure.

At the time of the winter solstice, the Romans celebrated Saturnalia, which were feast days devoted to Saturn (god of agriculture), Ops (goddess of plenty, aka Mother Earth), Consus (god of harvested grain), and Janus (god of beginnings and gates, from whom we got January). And what, pray tell, occurred during Saturnalia? Well, it was a *factio*—a party, of course. And since the Romans cooked their food over wood, what could be more appropriate than a barbecue to celebrate the winter solstice? See how this works? I bet most of you never celebrated the winter solstice before. Now you have a new excuse to barbecue.

Stuffed White Mushrooms

Craisined Pork Roast on a Plank

Stuffed Acorn Squash

Whiskey Peaches over Ice Cream

▼▼▼▼

Stuffed White Mushrooms

3 slices bacon

2 tablespoons olive oil

½ cup finely chopped onion

1 poblano pepper, roasted, peeled, seeds and stem removed, finely chopped

1 tablespoon minced sun-dried tomatoes, packed tightly (the dry ones)

1 clove garlic, crushed

½ cup vegetable or chicken broth

¼ cup seasoned breadcrumbs

½ cup freshly grated Parmesan cheese

Salt and freshly ground pepper to taste

1 pound whole white mushrooms, stems removed

Nowadays we have many exotic mushrooms readily available, so the regular old white mushrooms seem kind of boring to me. I figure they need a pretty intense stuffing. I like to use dried products when I feel that way, like dried apricots or sun-dried tomatoes, because they are so flavor packed. So this recipe started with white mushrooms and sun-dried tomatoes and just got built from there. When you buy sun-dried tomatoes, there are typically two kinds available. One will be in a jar in oil, and the other will be dry and packed in plastic like dried fruits. The second is usually my preference; you'll probably find them near the produce department. I also use the regular white mushrooms. The store may also have fancy stuffing mushrooms, which are all the same size and pretty. These are a little more expensive and they are fine. I kind of like the different sizes, though. Some guests may want a small one and some may want a larger one.

I find this to be a perfect recipe to use a separate grate-type thing that sits on top of the regular grate. These are usually sold as fish grills and come in different shapes and sizes. Some are disposable and some are heavy and coated with little holes all over. Any of them will work fine. What they do is allow you to place all the mushrooms on the grill quickly, and then when they are done you just remove the whole thing, mushrooms and all, just as quickly.

• **Yield: 6 to 8 servings**

In a medium nonstick skillet, cook the bacon over medium heat until crisp. Remove the bacon, drain, crumble, and reserve it. Add the olive oil to the bacon grease. Add the onion and sauté for about 2 minutes.

Add the poblano, the sun-dried tomatoes, and the garlic and cook another 2 minutes or until everything is soft. Add the bacon and the broth and cook another 2 minutes. Add the breadcrumbs and the Parmesan and remove the pan from the heat. Stir everything well. Check for salt and pepper and add as needed.

Let the stuffing mixture cool for about 10 minutes.

Prepare the grill for direct grilling at a medium-hot temperature.

With a spoon, stuff each mushroom very full. The stuffing should be mounded on top so the mushrooms look like they are wearing bad little toupees.

They now need to be grilled. If you're using a fish grill, set them all in position and put the whole thing on. If you're not, then place each one directly on the cooking grate. They will need to cook about 10 minutes over medium-high heat. Look for the filling to bubble, and they are done. The mushroom may get a little crunchy on the bottom, but that's okay. If you have one of those heavy fish grills, they may take a little longer.

Craisined Pork Roast on a Plank

1 boneless pork loin roast, 3 to 4 pounds, cut in a jelly-roll fashion

5 slices bacon

¼ cup finely chopped onion

1 cup Craisins (sweetened dried cranberries)

½ cup chopped walnuts

2 tablespoons butter

½ teaspoon salt

½ teaspoon finely ground black pepper

½ teaspoon rubbed sage

1 teaspoon lemon zest

1 tablespoon freshly squeezed lemon juice

3 tablespoons breadcrumbs

Dr. BBQ's Pork Seasoning (page 281)

Butcher string, or any cotton string

1 maple cooking plank, soaked in water for at least 1 hour (cedar will work)

Cooking on a plank is a great idea during the winter. It's a very forgiving way to cook indirectly. Just don't overcook the pork loin roast. • **Yield: 6 to 8 servings**

Cutting the pork roast is best done by a butcher, but if you've got a sharp knife and are a little adventurous you can do it. Just start on the bottom so you can hide the seam later. Take your time, cut all the way across the roast a little at a time, and unroll the roast as you go.

In a large skillet cook the bacon over medium heat until crisp. Remove the bacon, drain, crumble, and reserve it. Add the onion to the bacon fat. Cook for a minute or two, stirring occasionally, and then add the Craisins and the walnuts. Continue cooking until the onions are soft. Add the butter, salt, pepper, and sage. Cook just until the butter is melted, stirring constantly. Remove from the heat and add the lemon zest, lemon juice, and the crumbled bacon. Mix well. Add as much of the breadcrumbs as you need to soak up all the juices. Stir well. Transfer to a bowl and cool at room temp for at least 30 minutes.

Prepare the grill for direct grilling at a medium-high temperature.

Unroll the prepared pork roast. Sprinkle the inside liberally with Dr. BBQ's Pork Seasoning. Spread the stuffing evenly over most of the flat roast, just leaving a 1-inch border all around without stuffing. Roll the roast back up, trying to shape to a uniform thickness. Cut individual lengths of string and tie the roast every couple of inches. Do the 2 ends first to hold the stuffing in. Try to keeps the knots in a line for a nice presentation. Trim the loose ends of the string as close as you can with scissors. Season the outside of the roast liberally with Dr. BBQ's Pork Seasoning. Take the plank out of the water and put the roast directly on it. Put the plank and the roast directly on the grill.

The plank should get hot and even smoke as the heat dries it. Cook until the pork reaches an internal temperature of 145°F. This should take 1½ to 2 hours. Remove the whole plank to a baking sheet. Tent with foil and let rest 5 minutes. Carve and serve right from the plank.

Stuffed Acorn Squash

2 large acorn squashes

3 tablespoons olive oil

1 medium onion, chopped

1 green bell pepper, seeded and chopped

8 ounces white mushrooms, sliced

3 cloves garlic, crushed

One 14.5-ounce can diced tomatoes, drained

½ cup vegetable or chicken broth

1 tablespoon dried basil

1 teaspoon salt

½ teaspoon finely ground black pepper

¼ cup seasoned breadcrumbs

¼ cup freshly grated Parmesan cheese

I was lucky enough to be drawn as a participant in the "I Know Jack" grilling contest last year, a fun part of the Jack Daniel's World Championship Barbecue cookoff. Each contestant is given a new Fiesta Gas Grill and a bag of ingredients. You get a half hour to come up with a plan and you can use a couple of your own ingredients. One of the things in the bag was an acorn squash. So I quickly made a stuffing and put the whole thing on the grill and it came out beautifully. This is not exactly the recipe I made that day. It is, however, the recipe I would have made if I'd had the proper ingredients and a little more time. • **Yield: 6 to 8 servings**

Preheat the oven or prepare the grill for indirect grilling at 350°F. With a sharp knife, cut the tops off the squashes. Save the tops. With a spoon, clean out the cavity well. Cut the point off the bottom of the squashes so they will stand up straight. Lightly salt the inside of the squashes and set aside.

In a large skillet on medium heat, pour the olive oil. Let it heat for a minute or so and then add the onion and green pepper. Sauté for about 5 minutes, stirring occasionally. Add the mushrooms and garlic. Continue cooking, stirring occasionally, until the mushrooms get soft. Add the tomatoes, broth, basil, salt, and pepper and continue cooking until everything is hot and coming together. Remove from the heat and add the breadcrumbs and cheese. Blend well, adding additional broth if it looks too dry.

Stuff each squash with half the ingredients. Brush the top rim of the squash with olive oil.

Put the squashes in a pan and cook for about 1 hour, or until the flesh is soft when checked with a toothpick. I like to serve these whole with a big sturdy spoon, and suggest that the guests get some squash from the side along with their stuffing.

Whiskey Peaches over Ice Cream

½ stick butter

One 29-ounce can sliced peaches, drained

¼ cup brown sugar

1 ounce Jack Daniel's Tennessee Whiskey

4 bowls of chocolate or vanilla ice cream

• Yield: 4 servings

In a medium saucepan melt the butter over medium heat. Add the peaches and cook about 5 minutes, stirring occasionally. Add the brown sugar and continue cooking and stirring until the sauce evaporates to a point where you have more peaches than sauce. Remove from the heat and add the whiskey. Stir well. Spoon over the 4 bowls of ice cream.

Christmas:
Holiday Gift Grilling

▼▼

The tradition of giving gifts at Christmas goes back to the Three Wise Guys who brought gold, frankincense, and myrrh to the baby Jesus. Frankincense and myrrh are gum resins, not exactly a great gift in our time, so I have some better ideas. How about a remote wireless meat thermometer? Maverick makes a nice one that I use all the time. It's a wireless thermometer, timer, transmitter, and receiver set that allows you to keep track of food on the grill from up to one hundred feet away. You stick the transmitter probe in the meat and bring the receiver into the house. How's that for a nice winter barbecue tool? These things even have meat settings to tell you when, say, pork, is done, but you might want to determine if they agree with what you have in mind, as it's not always that simple. Some cuts of pork are best cooked to different temperatures than others. Those meat settings are easily ignored, and the actual temps can be used, too. It's a great grilling gadget gift for the barbecuer in the family and it only costs about fifty bucks.

Another temperature-taking tool that I have become really attached to is the Thermapen, made by a company named ThermoWorks. This thing is the ultimate hand-held food thermometer. It reads the temp in three to four seconds and is truly accurate. It's a little pricey, in the $85 range, but well worth it. Just be sure to get the superfast version. They only sell direct at http://www.thermoworks.com.

Here are some other Christmas gift ideas for the outdoor cook; they are easily found by doing a Web search:

- Cut-resistant gloves, perfect for the knife-challenged butcher wannabe

- Silicone basting brush. Silicone bristles make this brush heat resistant to 600°F, so it's perfect for the barbecue

- Clamp-on barbecue lamp. This is handy when you grill at night.

- Deluxe marinade injector—perfect for putting the flavor inside the meat

- Cedar or maple barbecue planks from my friend Gina Knox, who runs a great little company called Sautee Cedar

- Barbecue grill wok, the easiest way to grill vegetables, shrimp, and corn on the cob

- Silicone oven mitts, heat resistant to 500°F, protect your hands as you turn the steaks.

- A pizza stone for baking brick oven–style pizza and flat breads on the grill

All the gift giving can work up a big appetite and, of course, the whole gang should be gathered around, so I like to cook a big meal on Christmas with lots of choices.

Dr. BBQ's Crab Cakes

Christmas Standing Rib Roast

Dr. BBQ's Root Beer Carrots

Buttery Onion Rice

Austrian Walnut Whipped Cream Torte

▼▼▼▼

Dr. BBQ's Crab Cakes

1 egg, lightly beaten

¼ cup mayonnaise

1 teaspoon Louisiana hot sauce

1 teaspoon Worcestershire sauce

1 teaspoon dry mustard

1 teaspoon chopped parsley

½ teaspoon paprika

½ teaspoon salt

½ teaspoon coarsely ground black pepper

1 pound lump crab meat

1 cup seasoned breadcrumbs

¼ cup vegetable oil

¼ cup butter

Lemon wedges for garnish

Some things are best left alone. This is a traditional crab cake recipe, and it features the crab. I just couldn't imagine them any other way. • **Yield: 6 to 8 servings**

In a large bowl, combine the egg, mayo, hot sauce, Worcestershire sauce, and all the dry ingredients except the breadcrumbs. Blend well. Gently fold in the crab, taking great care to leave it as chunky as possible. Now add half the breadcrumbs and fold gently again. Continue adding breadcrumbs, just until the mixture is firm enough to be formed into patties; you may not have to use all the breadcrumbs.

Preheat a large skillet over medium heat and add the oil and butter. When it is hot, begin making patties and put them directly into the pan. You should get 6 to 8 patties, depending on how large you make them. Cook about 3 to 4 minutes until the bottom is golden brown, then flip and cook another 3 to 4 minutes until the second side is golden brown.

Remove to a paper towel for a short rest and to drain, about 1 to 2 minutes.

Transfer to plates and serve with lemon wedges and hot sauce on the side.

Christmas Standing Rib Roast

One 4-bone USDA Choice bone-in rib roast, bones removed and tied back on

½ cup Worcestershire sauce

Dr. BBQ's Steak Seasoning (page 282)

Standing rib roast is an old name for a bone-in beef rib roast. Nowadays, most folks cook a boneless rib-eye roast in place of the bone-in, mainly because they are much more available, and they are also easier to cook and carve. That said, the presentation of a bone-in roast is truly impressive, and they are available. I look for a true butcher and ask him to remove the bones and then tie them back on. This way you get the dramatic appearance, the rib bones for those who like them, but still have the ease of boneless carving. This is easy to do on the grill. There's a good reason to barbecue on Christmas. • **Yield: 6 to 8 servings**

Wet the roast all over with the Worcestershire sauce and then sprinkle liberally with the steak seasoning. Let rest, covered, at room temperature for 1 hour.

Prepare the grill for indirect grilling at 325°F, using cherrywood for flavor.

Place the roast directly on the grate, with the bones facing the most direct heat. Depending on your setup, you'll need to do one of a couple things. If you have a deflector right over the fire, simply put the bones facing down. If you have the fire in the same chamber as the food, but over to the side, just put the roast bones down directly over the fire for the first 5 minutes, and if you have an offset firebox, just turn the bone side toward the hot side for most of the cooking session.

To determine the doneness, take the temperature in the center of the roast. For rare it should be 125°F, for medium rare it should be 135°F. This should take approximately 15–20 minutes per pound. Anything beyond that, you are on your own. Remove to a platter and tent with foil. Let it rest for 15 minutes. Cut the string and remove the bones and cut them apart. Carve the roast thin or thick, depending on your preference.

Dr. BBQ's Root Beer Carrots

2 pounds carrots, peeled and cut into two-bite pieces

1 quart root beer

1 teaspoon salt

½ stick butter

¼ cup brown sugar

1 teaspoon coarsely ground black pepper

1 teaspoon Worcestershire sauce

I've been making these for years. It just all seemed like a good match to me. • **Yield: 6 servings**

In a large saucepan or Dutch oven, bring the carrots, the root beer, and the salt to a boil, then reduce to a strong simmer. Cook until the carrots are just tender, about 15 to 20 minutes. The liquid will reduce, but that's what you want. Add a little more root beer, but only if it's absolutely necessary.

When the carrots are tender, drain them, reserving the liquid. Return the carrots to the pan on the heat. Add the butter, brown sugar, black pepper, Worcestershire, and ¼ cup of the reserved cooking liquid. Stir well and cook until the liquid turns to a glaze and sticks to the carrots. This should take 5 to 7 minutes.

Buttery Onion Rice

3 tablespoons olive oil

1 stick butter

1 medium onion, sliced thin

4 cups cooked white rice

I made this for myself one day and realized it was pretty good and should be in a cookbook. Now it is.

• **Yield: 6 to 8 servings**

In a small frying pan over medium heat, combine the oil and butter. When the mixture is hot, add the onion. Cook, stirring occasionally, until the onion is browned and cooked through.

Put the fresh cooked rice in a large bowl. Pour the butter mixture over the top. Mix well and serve.

Austrian Walnut Whipped Cream Torte

6 eggs, separated

¾ cup sugar

¾ cup breadcrumbs

¾ cup finely ground walnuts

1 teaspoon vanilla flavoring

1 pint heavy cream, whipped until stiff peaks form

Ground walnuts for the garnish (optional)

This recipe is a gift from my friend Mary Jane Wilan, and it comes from the vast files of her grandmother, who would whip up an enormous apple strudel on a moment's notice. Although this dessert looks rich, it is surprisingly light and refreshing, probably because of the breadcrumbs. • **Yield: 8 servings**

Preheat the oven to 350°F.

Beat the egg yolks with the sugar for 15 minutes until the mixture is light and frothy. In a separate bowl, beat the egg whites until they are stiff.

Alternately fold the egg whites and breadcrumbs into the yolk mixture. Then fold in the ground nuts and the vanilla.

Pour the mixture into two 8-inch ungreased cake pans, dividing it evenly. Bake at 350°F for 30 minutes.

Remove the cakes from the oven and allow them to cool before removing them from the pans. When the cakes are cool, run a sharp knife around the pan edges and use a spatula to loosen the bottom of the cakes. Invert back onto cooling racks.

Cut each layer in half horizontally with a serrated knife. Place 1 of the halves onto a cake plate and spread with about ½ inch of the whipped cream. Place another layer on top of the first and spread with the whipped cream, and repeat with the other 2 layers. When all the layers are filled, frost the sides of the cake with the whipped cream and smooth the top. Additional ground nuts can be sprinkled over the top and sides of the cake, if desired.

Cover loosely and refrigerate for an hour or two to let the cake set and make slicing easier.

New Year's Eve:
The Ultimate Revelry

▼▼▼

It's a known fact that most grilling aficionados drink alcoholic beverages. And since New Year's Eve is traditionally the time for imbibing such drinks, I thought I would discuss which drinks go best with barbecue. This discussion assumes that you are partying at home and are not driving, or that you have a sober friend who will put up with you and drive you around.

I looked in the *Jack Daniel's Old Time Barbecue Cookbook* and guess what I found? About fifty drink recipes and all but three featured Jack Daniel's whiskey! I think maybe there's an agenda going on in Lynchburg. My favorite was Lynchburg Coonhunter's Punch. I'd put the sharp knives away before I started drinking this one. It calls for a bottle of brandy, a half-bottle of rum, four liters of champagne, and a bottle of Jack Daniel's. Now *that's* a drink.

Wine can be a good barbecue drink, too. In general zinfandels are considered a good choice to serve with barbecue. On a recent visit to the Seghesio winery in Sonoma Valley, I realized that the whole California zinfandel industry is embracing barbecue with their wines. I was there with Chris Lilly to cook hundreds of slabs of ribs to pair with the wine at a party. The Seghesio family makes some amazing wine, and the match with the ribs was perfect. The wine complemented the ribs without overwhelming the flavor of the spice. Of course a balls-out red with a grilled steak or something white with fish is always appropriate, too. Ask the guy at the wine store for a suggestion. Those guys like showing off and always give you a good selection. Tell them you are interested in a big value (read "good deal").

Of course, the number one drink with barbecue is beer. It's definitely the most popular beverage at cookoffs. This really shouldn't be a surprise. It comes in the handy single-serving aluminum container and is refreshing while you're working over a hot fire. I have researched this subject for many years. If they had beer guys in the liquor store like wine guys, I could be one. Lately I have also taken to drinking hard lemonade. This is sometimes referred to as cheerleader beer. It's really refreshing on a hot day. Then I went to Canada and found a product called Dave's Spiked Lemonade. Man, that stuff is good. They put more alcohol in the beer in Canada, too. My friend John Ford from Detroit regularly drives there to get this higher-alcohol beer. Occasionally, he stops at the Windsor Ballet while he's there, too. It's a little different from the typical ballet. There is usually a brass pole onstage and a scary doorman.

Last but not least, we must ask what James Beard has to say about the subject. I checked

Barbecue with Beard (1975) and found all the great summer cocktail standards: bloody mary, daiquiri, mint julep, planter's punch, whiskey sour, and Tom Collins. Those all sound good to me too. So it seems that the drinks served with barbecue are all over the map. Pick one and enjoy. Here's a toast to the New Year from Dr. BBQ!

Tom Collins

Smoky Swiss Cheese Fondue

Toasted Ravioli

Chipotle Black Bean Soup with Pumpkin

Rack of Pork

Grilled Zucchini-Mushroom Kabobs

Dr. BBQ's Crème Brûlée

Tom Collins

2 ounces gin

Juice of ½ lemon

1 teaspoon castor sugar, aka superfine sugar

3 to 4 ounces club soda

Maraschino cherries and orange slices for garnish

This is a classic drink that most people will enjoy at a party. You should probably have some beer and wine too for the less adventurous guests. • **Yield: 1 serving**

In a large glass or a cocktail shaker combine the gin, lemon juice, and sugar. Mix well or shake thoroughly. Strain into a glass half-filled with ice. Top with club soda and garnish with a cherry and an orange slice.

Smoky Swiss Cheese Fondue

½ pound Emmental cheese, grated

1 pound Gruyère cheese, grated

3 tablespoons cornstarch

1½ cups dry white wine

1 teaspoon coarsely ground black pepper

1 tablespoon Tabasco sauce

Pinch of ground nutmeg

Salt to taste

2 loaves of French bread, cubed

I was a young adult during the '70s, and I'm pretty sure my mom had a fondue pot during their first appearance in the United States, but I had other things on my mind in those days so I'm not sure if she ever even fired it up. Nowadays, I do enjoy a fondue as a nice friendly dinner. Of course, my smoky version is another excuse to fire up the grill and have this ready to serve with drinks as your guests arrive. If you don't have a fondue pot, just use a saucepan and bamboo skewers. • **Yield: 6 to 8 servings**

Prepare the grill for indirect cooking at 200°F, using apple wood for flavor.

Spread the cheeses out on a low-sided pan and place in the cooker for 15 minutes.

Meanwhile, in a bowl, whisk the cornstarch with the wine, and pour the mixture into a warm fondue pot. Stir in the black pepper and the Tabasco sauce.

After 15 minutes get the cheese from the cooker and add it to the fondue pot. Stir occasionally until it's well blended and warm. Add the nutmeg and check for salt and pepper, adding if needed. Serve with bread cubes.

Toasted Ravioli

Vegetable oil for frying

1½ cups all-purpose flour

1 teaspoon salt

¾ cup milk

2 eggs, lightly beaten

1½ cups Italian seasoned breadcrumbs

1 package (26 ounces) frozen cheese ravioli, thawed

Freshly grated Parmesan cheese

2 cups marinara sauce for dipping

This is a favorite dish in the Italian area of St. Louis and another nice appetizer to offer your guests before dinner. Once you try it, you'll surely understand why. I use frozen ravioli and marinara sauce from a jar; I think Paul Newman's Own is very good sauce for this purpose. If you have a favorite homemade recipe for the ravioli or sauce, be sure to substitute them.

• **Yield: 6 to 8 servings as an appetizer or side dish**

Heat the oil in a Dutch oven to 350°F; it must be at least 2 inches deep.

Combine the flour and salt in a bowl, combine the milk and eggs in another bowl, and put the breadcrumbs in a third bowl.

Roll each ravioli around in the flour, then dip in the egg wash, and finally coat fully with the breadcrumbs. Rest them on a cake rack until all are done.

Fry them a few at a time until golden brown, about 2 to 3 minutes per batch. Don't put too many in the oil at a time and be sure the temp gets back to 350°F before starting the next batch.

Drain on paper towels, then transfer all of the ravioli to a big warm platter to serve. Sprinkle with Parmesan and drizzle with a small amount of the marinara. Serve the rest of the marinara on the side for dipping.

Chipotle Black Bean Soup with Pumpkin

1 pound black beans

Water to cover

1 teaspoon salt

¾ cup drained canned tomatoes

1 cup canned unsweetened pumpkin puree

2 to 3 chipotle chiles, rehydrated in hot water and chopped

3 cups chicken stock

¼ cup vegetable oil

1½ cups finely chopped onion

3 cloves garlic, peeled and crushed

1 teaspoon ground cumin

¼ cup red wine vinegar

½ cup medium sherry

Cilantro leaves for garnish

What is it about the combination of black beans and chipotle chiles? They just seem to work together perfectly, and a little pumpkin helps to firm up this spicy soup. It takes a bit of time to cook the beans, but after that it's a snap. • **Yield: 8 servings**

In a large saucepan, combine the beans, water to cover plus 2 inches, and the salt. Bring to a boil, partially cover the pan, reduce the heat, and simmer until the beans are tender, 1½ to 2 hours. Drain the beans.

Stir the tomatoes into the beans and transfer to a food processor. Pulse briefly, leaving the beans somewhat chunky. Return the beans and tomatoes to the saucepan and stir in the pumpkin, chipotles, and half the stock. Bring to a simmer.

Heat the oil over medium heat in a saucepan. Add the onions and sauté for about 8 minutes. Add the garlic and cumin and stir well. Add this onion mixture to the beans, stir in the remaining stock and the vinegar, and simmer for 15 minutes. Adjust the consistency by adding sherry, and stir well.

Serve garnished with the cilantro leaves.

Rack of Pork

1 rack of pork roast, about 4 pounds

2 cloves garlic, cut into slivers

Dr. BBQ's Pork Seasoning (page 281)

This cut is simply a boneless pork loin roast with the rib bones attached. You may need to find a real butcher to make one for you. The meat should be trimmed, or frenched, from the ends of the bones for a really nice presentation. You can even get those frilly things to decorate them. The preparation is simple and delicious.

• Yield: 6 to 8 servings

Prepare the grill for indirect cooking at 300°F, using apple wood for flavor.

With a pointy knife stab the roast and stick a sliver of garlic in the slit. Do this randomly all over the roast. Season the roast liberally with Dr. BBQ's Pork Seasoning.

Place the roast directly on the grate and cook until it reaches an internal temp of 150°F. This should take about 2½ hours.

Remove to a platter, tent with foil, and let rest for 15 minutes before carving.

If you are a little adventurous, try an internal temp of 145°F. But be warned that it may be a little pink. This is safely cooked, but many guests are bothered by it.

Grilled Zucchini-Mushroom Kabobs

4 teaspoons red chile powder

¼ cup chile oil

2 tablespoons cider vinegar

1 tablespoon freshly squeezed lemon juice

Freshly ground black pepper

2 zucchini, cut into ½-inch slices

1 small purple onion, cut into wedges

16 mushroom caps

Bamboo skewers, soaked in water for 1 hour

3 tablespoons freshly grated Parmesan cheese

Zucchini works well for these vegetable kabobs, but you can experiment with vegetables such as eggplants, other squashes, and even corn on the cob. • **Yield: 4 servings**

Combine the chile pepper, chile oil, vinegar, lemon juice, and black pepper in a bowl. Put the zucchini, onion, and mushrooms in a zip bag. Pour the marinade over the vegetables. Refrigerate for 1 to 2 hours.

Prepare the grill for direct grilling at high heat.

Thread the vegetables on skewers and grill, basting frequently with the marinade and turning them often. The vegetables should take 12 to 15 minutes.

When they are just about ready to take off the grill, brush the kabobs with the marinade, sprinkle with the cheese, and grill until the cheese is lightly browned.

Dr. BBQ's Crème Brûlée

3 cups heavy cream

1 tablespoon pure vanilla extract

1 ounce whiskey

7 egg yolks

⅔ cup sugar

½ cup brown sugar for topping

½ cup chopped pecans for garnish

What a great finish this is to the New Year's Eve celebration! • **Yield: 6 to 8 servings**

Preheat the oven to 325°F.

In a heavy saucepan, bring the cream to a simmer but do not boil. Remove from the heat and mix in the vanilla and whiskey. Transfer to a double boiler with gently simmering water.

In a bowl beat the egg yolks and the sugar until smooth. Add a little of the cream mixture to the eggs, stirring constantly to blend. Do this a couple of times so the eggs get tempered and don't turn to scrambled eggs. If by chance they do, you'll have to start over. There is no way to salvage cooked eggs. Now pour the tempered egg mixture into the cream mixture in the double boiler. Cook for about 10 to 15 minutes, stirring constantly, until the mixture thickens and coats the back of a spoon.

Pour into 6 to 8 ramekins. Place them in a pan and add hot water to go halfway up the sides of the ramekins. Bake for about 35 minutes, until the custard is set.

Remove the ramekins to a rack to cool. After 30 minutes cover them in plastic wrap and refrigerate for at least 6 hours, or preferably overnight.

Right before serving, sprinkle the tops of all the custards with brown sugar and brown under a hot broiler, or use a hot little crème brûlée torch, available at any kitchen store. As soon as the tops are browned, sprinkle with the pecans. Let rest for 5 to 10 minutes so the sugar will get crunchy.

New Year's Day:
Traditions

▼▼

The start of the New Year is all about luck. My mom always ate herring on New Year's Day. As a kid I remember the adult men sitting at the kitchen table with coffee and whiskey. I guess that was lucky for them. In our French family their drink was called a Beestool. I apologize to the French language for the spelling. The tradition in Spain at the end of New Year's Eve is to eat twelve grapes for good luck. As the clock strikes midnight, you should eat one grape at each toll of the bell. I think this is also where the Heimlich maneuver was invented. In Austria, the traditional food is pork because the pig roots forward. Lobster is avoided there because it moves backward. The Brazilians eat lentils on New Year's Day because they symbolize good luck.

Here are some other international lucky foods eaten to promote prosperity and happiness:

- Scotland: haggis (I still can't believe this is a real thing that people eat)

- Norway: rice pudding with almonds

- Bahamas: corn fritters

- Sicily: lentils and sausage

- Jamaica: curried goat

- Nigeria: yams and pumpkin

- Russia: hot borscht

In the United States, the tradition of lucky food is strong in the South, where a certain saying goes, "Eat poor on New Year's, eat fat the rest of the year." Ham and pork are considered to be lucky, as is cornbread. Black-eyed peas are thought to bring wealth because they resemble little coins, and tradition has it that collard or turnip greens bring good fortune for the year because they are the color of money. In Louisiana, pork brings good health, and cabbage brings wealth. Of course there is no scientific evidence that any of this is true, but they are fun traditions, and besides, you never know.

Here's my lucky New Year's Southern barbecue meal.

Classic Mimosa

Smoked Catfish Spread

Smoked Catfish

Pulled Pork Sandwiches with Ed's Red Slaw

Traditional Southern Greens

Hoppin' John with Smoked Ham Hocks

Confederate Cornbread

Whiskey Pralines

▼▼▼▼

Classic Mimosa

4 champagne flutes

1 cup orange juice or more
to taste

1 bottle champagne or
other sparkling white
wine

4 slices fresh orange for
garnish

A toast on New Year's Day should involve champagne, and this is my favorite champagne "mixed drink."

• Yield: 4 servings

Fill each flute one-quarter full of orange juice, top off with champagne, and garnish with the orange slices.

Smoked Catfish Spread

1 pound catfish fillets, smoked (recipe follows)

½ cup mayonnaise

¼ cup cream cheese, softened

1 tablespoon Louisiana hot sauce

1 teaspoon dried chives

Zest of 1 lemon

Because of the catfish farmers and their fine organization, the Catfish Institute, this tasty white fish is readily available all over the country. But any white fish will work in this recipe. • **Yield: 6 to 8 servings**

Crumble the catfish by hand into a bowl. Add the mayo and mix. Add the cream cheese and mix. Add the rest of the ingredients and mix well until the color and texture are consistent. Serve on crackers of choice with champagne or a mimosa (page 26).

Smoked Catfish

1 pound catfish fillets

For this spread I don't season the catfish at all and I cook it to a well-done state.

• Yield: 4 servings

Note: This recipe is best done the day before you plan to make the spread.

Prepare the grill for indirect cooking at 250°F, using pecan wood for flavor. Prepare a double-thick piece of aluminum foil a little larger than the fillets will need. Fold the edges under and spray it with a vegetable oil spray. Put the foil on the grate of the grill.

Cut the fillets in half and place on the foil. Cook for about 2 hours or until very firm. Remove to a plate to cool. Cover and refrigerate until chilled.

Pulled Pork Sandwiches with Ed's Red Slaw

One 7- to 8-pound pork butt, bone in

Year-Round Barbecue Rub (page 277)

Dr. BBQ's Pork Mop (page 298)

1 cup Dr. BBQ's Race Day Barbecue Sauce (page 285) mixed with 1 cup apple juice

12 fluffy white buns

Ed's Red Slaw (recipe follows)

If pork brings good luck, then slow-smoked pulled pork must bring lotto winners. For me, this is what true-blue barbecue is all about. It's just the perfect combination of fat to meat, and the shape of a butt is just right to create the right ratio of crusty bark to soft and moist inside meat. Toss it all together with a little barbecue sauce and apple juice mixture and it's nirvana. Many people insist that slaw belongs on the pork sandwich. It's not my preference, but all those folks can't be wrong, so I've included a great red slaw recipe from one of my early barbecue mentors, Ed Roith. This pork makes great leftovers and can be used as a part of many other dishes, such as my Pulled Pork Stuffing that I serve on Thanksgiving (page 265), so you may want to make two. It's best to pull it apart before freezing. The best way to package it is to use a Foodsaver vacuum machine. Those things work great. • **Yield: About 12 servings**

I really don't trim anything off the butt unless I find something weird on the outside. I pack the rub on as heavily as I can in the exposed meat areas. No need to season the fat cap. Return it to the refrigerator for at least 30 minutes but up to 12 hours.

Prepare the grill for indirect cooking at 235°F, using two-thirds cherry and one-third hickory for flavor.

Put the butt in fat side down. Cook for 6 hours before even peeking. After 6 hours, mop the meat, and then mop it again at 8 hours. After that, mop and check it every hour until it reaches an internal temp of 190°F. If the bone is sticking out and the meat feels soft, it is done. If it's still a little tough, cook it a little longer but not past 200°F.

Take it out of the cooker, tent it with foil, and let it rest for 30 minutes. With big neoprene gloves or two forks, just slide what is left of the fat cap off and discard it. Slide the bone out and discard it. Now just go through the butt, shredding the good meat and discarding any fat. Toss the meat all together with a little more rub and the barbecue sauce–apple juice mixture. Pile high on the buns and top with the slaw.

Ed's Red Slaw

A Recipe from Barbecue All Star Ed Roith

When I was getting started as a serious competition barbecue cook, there were quite a few people that I truly looked up to as the pioneers of the game. Some of these folks were there at the original cookoffs, and others came along a little later, but they all shared the passion for this great hobby. Now it's many years later and I know most of those people. It's interesting to look back at how they helped things get to where they are now. One name that comes to mind, as a legend in the world of competition barbecue and an early mentor of mine, is Ed Roith. Ed and his late wife, Muriel, personally helped me many times, and there are lots of today's top cooks that will tell you the same story. When they cooked as Happy Holla' they were among the elite in any cookoff they entered. They won many of the biggest awards in the country, despite their career being cut short by Muriel's passing. Ed stopped cooking after that, but he remains an active member of the barbecue community. Ed taught the first barbecue cooking class I ever attended. It was amazing how many things he shared that nobody in that room knew before that day.

Muriel helped just about every team she ever met with tips on handling the presentation of the food. She was truly one of the best at that. Ed also pioneered the Kansas City Barbeque Society's Certified Barbecue Judging (CBJ) program and continues to be the force behind it. When I think of Barbecue All Stars, Ed Roith is at the top of the list,

1 head cabbage, about 2 pounds, cored and sliced thin

1 cup ketchup

½ cup cider vinegar

½ cup barbecue sauce of choice

½ cup white sugar

½ tablespoon salt

½ tablespoon finely ground black pepper

and I thank him for sharing this recipe with me. It is great as a side dish or as a topping for a pulled pork sandwich.

• **Yield: At least 12 servings**

Put the cabbage in a big plastic or glass bowl. In a second bowl, mix together the ketchup, vinegar, and barbecue sauce. Blend in the sugar and salt and pepper. Pour over the sliced cabbage and mix thoroughly. Refrigerate for 8 to 24 hours.

Note: Adjust the vinegar, sugar, salt, and pepper to taste after refrigeration, if needed. The slaw may seem too dry when first mixed, but after a few hours it will become very moist.

Traditional Southern Greens

¼ **pound bacon, sliced**

2 **quarts water**

1 **teaspoon salt**

½ **teaspoon dried crushed red pepper**

5 **pounds greens, trimmed and rinsed**

2 **turnips, peeled and sliced (optional)**

You can use collard, mustard, or turnip greens in this recipe or a mixture of all three. Southern greens are served with vinegar and/or hot pepper sauce, raw chopped onions, and, of course, cornbread (Confederate Cornbread, page 35). • **Yield: 6 to 8 servings**

Cook the bacon in a large stockpot until almost crisp. Remove, reserving 2 teaspoons of the drippings in the pot. Crumble the bacon and set aside.

Bring the water, salt, and red pepper to boil in the stockpot. Add the greens, a few at a time. Add the turnips if desired.

Sprinkle the bacon on top of the greens. Cover and cook over medium heat for 45 to 60 minutes or until tender.

Hoppin' John with Smoked Ham Hocks

2 cups black-eyed peas or pigeon peas

6 cups water

¾ cup chopped onion

¼ cup chopped celery

2 pounds smoked ham hocks

1 cup uncooked brown rice

¼ teaspoon freshly ground black pepper

This is a traditional New Year's Day dish in the South. There are almost as many theories as to how Hoppin' John got its name as there are ways to cook the dish. One story attributes the name to the custom of inviting guests to eat with, "Hop in, John." Another suggestion is that it is derived from an old ritual on New Year's Day in which the children of the house hopped once around the table before eating the dish. Whatever its origin, it was definitely a staple for many in the early South and remains an important dish today. • **Yield: 6 to 8 servings**

In a large bowl, soak the peas in the water overnight.

Transfer the peas and the soaking liquid to a large pot and add the onion, celery, and ham hocks. Cover and cook over medium heat until the peas are tender but still whole, about 45 minutes. Add the rice and pepper, cover, and simmer for about 1 hour, or until the rice is cooked.

Remove the meat from the ham hocks and discard the bones and fat. Mix the meat into the peas and rice. Serve hot.

Confederate Cornbread

1 cup cornmeal

¾ cup all-purpose flour

2½ teaspoons baking powder

¾ teaspoon salt

¼ teaspoon baking soda

1 cup buttermilk

3 tablespoons melted butter

1 egg, lightly beaten

1½ teaspoons vegetable oil

I know people who add chopped jalapeños to this recipe; it's not Southern traditional, but it sure is good.

• **Yield: 6 to 8 servings**

Preheat the oven to 425°F. In a bowl, combine all the ingredients except the vegetable oil. Grease a 10-inch cast-iron skillet with the vegetable oil and heat it on top of the stove until it is very hot. Pour the batter into the hot skillet and bake for 15 to 20 minutes.

Whiskey Pralines

1 cup chopped pecans

¼ cup heavy cream

¼ cup (½ stick) unsalted butter

1 cup plus 2 tablespoons light brown sugar

1 teaspoon vanilla extract

1 tablespoon whiskey (Old No. 7 is my choice)

Here is one of my favorite Southern desserts that's flavored with one of my favorite Southern beverages. • **Yield: About 24 pralines**

Preheat the oven to 325°F.

Spread the pecans on a cookie sheet and place in the oven for 3 minutes. For even toasting, turn the tray front to back. Toss the nuts with a metal spatula and bake for another 3 minutes. Take care that they do not burn.

Line a cookie sheet with baking parchment.

Fit a heavy-bottomed saucepan with a candy thermometer. Over high heat, cook the cream, butter, and brown sugar to 240°F (soft ball stage). If necessary, stir once to help dissolve the sugar. Remove from the heat and let sit for 15 seconds.

Carefully stir in the vanilla, whiskey, and toasted pecans. Vigorously stir with a spoon for 10 seconds, until the mixture looks creamy and slightly thickened. Drop by tablespoonfuls onto the prepared cookie sheet.

Let cool for 20 minutes.

Groundhog Day:
Fair and Bright

▼▼

The origin of this tradition goes back to Candlemas Day, which I looked up on the Internet and found out that it's the last festival in the Christian year and comes forty days after Christmas, on February 2. There's an old English song that goes:

If Candlemas be fair and bright,
Come winter, have another flight.

The legend was transferred to Punxsutawney, Pennsylvania, in 1886, when *The Punxsutawney Spirit* wrote, "Today is the groundhog's day, and up to the time of going to press the beast has not seen his shadow." If he had seen his shadow at Gobbler's Knob, where his burrow is, legend holds that there would have been six more weeks of winter. The famed woodchuck, now known as Punxsutawney Phil, gets his longevity from a "groundhog punch" that he sips during a summer picnic and that magically gives him seven more years of life.

So, if Phil sees his shadow, here's a winter menu for celebrating this hallowed but chilly day.

Grilled Corn Soup

Grilled Rabbit

Grilled Chile Vegetables

Apple Crisp with Raisins and Vanilla Yogurt Topping

▼▼▼▼

Grilled Corn Soup

4 ears frozen corn, defrosted

2 cloves garlic, minced

½ cup finely chopped carrots

½ cup finely chopped onion

¼ cup finely chopped celery

1 jalapeño chile, seeds and stem removed, minced

1½ cups chicken stock

1 cup half-and-half

Cilantro leaves for garnish

This is a great grilled soup to keep you warm during those six extra weeks of winter. • **Yield: 4 servings**

Grill the ears of corn for 5 minutes over a hot flame, turning often. Remove, cool, and cut the kernels from the ears.

Combine the corn, garlic, carrots, onions, celery, jalapeño, and stock in a pan and simmer for 30 minutes.

Add the half-and-half, bring to a boil, and boil for 5 minutes.

Remove from the heat and serve garnished with the cilantro leaves.

Grilled Rabbit

½ cup vegetable oil, peanut preferred

3 tablespoons chopped green onions

2 cloves garlic, chopped

2 teaspoons freshly ground black pepper

½ teaspoon ground cumin

½ teaspoon ground cayenne pepper

½ teaspoon dried rosemary

½ teaspoon dried thyme

¼ teaspoon dried oregano

One 2-pound rabbit, cut into serving pieces

Even though you might want to grill Phil for giving you six more weeks of winter, I'd personally substitute a rabbit and just pretend he's Phil. Rabbit is a great lean meat, and I've included a recipe for a marinade that will help keep the meat from drying out during the grilling. • **Yield: 4 to 6 servings**

Prepare the grill for direct grilling over high heat.

In a large bowl combine all the ingredients for the marinade and stir well. Add the rabbit and marinate for at least 3 hours, covered, in the refrigerator.

Remove the meat from the bowl and grill over a hot fire for about 7 minutes per side until cooked to medium.

Grilled Chile Vegetables

½ cup olive oil

2 cloves garlic, minced

1 teaspoon red chile powder

3 small zucchini, cut into 1-inch slices

2 onions, peeled and cut into quarters

8 cherry tomatoes

3 medium crookneck squashes, cut into 1-inch cubes

8 large button mushrooms

Feel free to substitute other favorite veggies for the ones listed here. • **Yield: 6 servings**

Prepare the grill for direct grilling over medium heat.

Whisk the olive oil, garlic, and red chile together in a large bowl.

Add the zucchini, onions, tomatoes, squash, and mushrooms and toss to coat the vegetables. Marinate at room temperature for 30 minutes.

Thread the vegetables on metal skewers, alternating the different types. Place the skewers on the grill over medium-hot coals; grill for about 15 minutes, basting frequently with the marinade and turning often.

Apple Crisp with Raisins and Vanilla Yogurt Topping

¾ cup fresh whole-wheat breadcrumbs

¼ cup firmly packed dark brown sugar

¾ teaspoon ground cinnamon

¼ teaspoon ground allspice

6 large baking apples (about 2½ pounds), peeled, cored, and sliced ½ inch thick

½ cup raisins

1 tablespoon freshly squeezed lemon juice

⅓ cup cider

2 tablespoons unsalted butter, chilled and cut into small pieces

1 cup vanilla yogurt

1 tablespoon honey

¼ teaspoon nutmeg

U se baking apples for this recipe; I like Granny Smith or Rome Beauty. You can serve the crisp with whipped cream, of course, but I've come up with another option. • **Yield: 6 servings**

Preheat the oven to 375°F.

In a bowl, combine the breadcrumbs, sugar, cinnamon, and allspice. In another bowl, combine the apples and raisins and toss with the lemon juice.

Spray a 2½-quart baking dish with vegetable cooking spray. Place half the apple mixture in the dish and pour the cider over it. Dot with half the butter and sprinkle with half the breadcrumb mixture. Add the remaining apples, then top with the remaining butter and crumb mixture.

Bake uncovered until the crumbs are golden brown, about 35 minutes.

In a bowl, combine the yogurt, honey, and nutmeg. Serve the crisp warm, topped with the yogurt.

Groundhog Day:
Clouds and Rain

▼▼

reatest Groundhog Day moments:

1887: This is the first official observance.

1921: During Prohibition, Phil threatens 60 weeks of winter if he doesn't get a drink.

1958: Phil says that the first manmade satellite was not Sputnik but Chucknik.

1981: Phil wears a yellow ribbon to honor the American hostages in Iran.

1986: Phil travels to Washington, D.C., and meets with President Reagan.

1993: Columbia Pictures releases *Groundhog Day*.

1994: Record crowds up to 30,000 strong appear at Gobbler's Knob because of the movie.

1995: Phil appears on the *Oprah Winfrey* show.

2001: Phil's prediction is shown live on the JumboTron at Times Square in New York City.

Now the old English song continues:

If Candlemas brings clouds and rain,
Go, winter, and not come again.

So if Phil doesn't see his shadow, spring is on the way, and here's a tropical menu that celebrates Phil's gift of nice warm weather.

Grilled Brie Quesadillas with Que-ribbean Salsa

Jerk-Smoked Chicken

Grilled Summer Squash with Lemon Garlic Marinade

Rummy Bananas with Nutmeg Whipped Cream

▼▼▼▼▼

Grilled Brie Quesadillas with Que-ribbean Salsa

1 to 2 tablespoons vegetable oil

Four 8-inch flour tortillas

8 ounces Brie cheese, rinds removed, cut in wide strips, or

8 ounces goat cheese, crumbled

Que-ribbean Salsa (page 290)

Quesadillas are usually fried, but I like these done on the grill with a tropical salsa. You might cut down on the amount of habanero if you're scared of the hot stuff.

• **Yield: 4 servings**

Prepare the barbecue grill for direct grilling over medium heat.

Place one-quarter of the cheese on half of each tortilla. Top with the salsa mixture and fold the tortilla in half.

Brush the top of the quesadillas with a little of the remaining oil and place them on the grill, oiled side down. Cook for a minute, brush the top with oil, and turn and cook for an additional minute.

Cut each quesadilla in thirds, arrange on a plate, top with Que-ribbean Salsa.

Jerk-Smoked Chicken

One 2- to 3-pound chicken, cut into serving pieces

Groundhog Jerk Seasoning (page 280)

Y ou're not going to be angry with Phil for saying, "Spring's on the way!" So let's have a chicken and give the guy a break. • **Yield: 4 to 6 servings**

Prepare the grill for indirect cooking over medium heat, using oak wood for flavoring.

In a bowl, combine all the ingredients for the rub and mix well. Rub the chicken all over with the jerk seasoning and allow to stand at room temperature, covered, for 1 hour.

Place the rubbed chicken pieces on the grate, close the lid, and smoke for about 4 hours.

Grilled Summer Squash with Lemon Garlic Marinade

3 medium yellow squash, cut into ¼-inch rounds

3 medium zucchini, cut into ¼-inch rounds

Lemon Garlic Marinade (page 294)

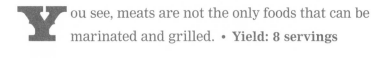ou see, meats are not the only foods that can be marinated and grilled. • **Yield: 8 servings**

Place the squash and zucchini in a large zip bag. Pour the marinade over the squash and marinate for at least 3 hours.

Prepare the grill for cooking at high heat.

Cook the squash over a very hot grill, to mark the vegetables on each side. The squash is done when it is tender but still crisp. Remove from the heat and serve.

Rummy Bananas
with Nutmeg Whipped Cream

The Bananas

½ cup brown sugar

¼ cup dark rum

1 teaspoon soy sauce

2 teaspoons freshly
squeezed lime juice

2 teaspoons melted butter

4 small firm bananas,
peeled and sliced
lengthwise

The Whipped Cream

½ cup heavy cream

2 tablespoons
confectioner's sugar

1 teaspoon rum

Grated nutmeg for garnish

Remember, the firmer the banana, the better it cooks. You can start this dessert while eating the entrée, and it will be ready when you are. You can just use aluminum foil over the grill rather than the aluminum pan, if you wish. • **Yield: 4 servings**

Prepare the grill for indirect cooking at medium heat.

In a bowl, combine the sugar, rum, soy sauce, lime juice, and butter. Arrange the bananas in a single layer in a disposable aluminum pan and drizzle the rum mixture over the top.

Set the pan on the grill over a medium fire, cover, and cook for 10 minutes, basting frequently with the sauce. Continue to grill until the bananas are glazed and tender, about another 5 to 10 minutes.

Prepare the cream by whipping the cream, sugar, and rum together in a cold bowl until stiff.

To serve, place the bananas on individual serving plates, drizzle a teaspoon of the remaining sauce over them, top with a dollop of whipped cream, and garnish with the grated nutmeg.

Super Bowl Barbecue:
A Super 'Cue Party

▼▼▼

I wanted my Super Bowl party to be the best ever, so I went to Party Planners of Lakeland and spoke with the owner, Janet. For a crisp $100 bill, she agreed to give me the meaning of life, along with some suggestions to create the perfect football-themed party.

"First," she told me, "you'll need a wreath on your front door decorated with the teams' colors and tiny footballs. That greets the guests and puts them in the proper mood." Then she suggested a unique tablecloth—green felt with yard lines marked with white chalk. But wait, there's more.

"A football surrounded by cut mums makes a nice centerpiece," she said, and advised me to wash the football first with a strong detergent. "And pom-poms make great wall decorations."

"Where do I find pom-poms?" I asked her.

"Oh, any cheerleaders' supply store will have them." (This was a stop I'd been meaning to make anyway.)

"And what about the food?"

"Pizza. Everyone loves pizza. Top them with pieces of sausage cut in the shape of footballs."

I was starting to get nervous and wondered what my buddies would think of all of this, but Janet was not finished.

"For dessert, I suggest a sheet cake football field. Green frosting, of course, with the team names in the end zones in white frosting. Use stick pretzels for the goalposts."

That did it. I howled with laughter and Janet gave me a hard look.

"What's so funny?" she asked, but I had already hightailed it out of there, on my way to the cheerleader store.

I ended up decorating the house with coolers of beer, and the food was lots of appetizers and an easy make-ahead main course so that everyone could watch the game. Not a football-decorated pizza in sight.

Dr. BBQ's Wings with Pantry Sauce

Rib Meat Potato Skins

Gyro Meatballs

Queso Q'dido

Alfredo Lasagna with Smoked Chicken

Super Garlic Bread

▼▼▼▼

Dr. BBQ's Wings with Pantry Sauce

12 whole chicken wings, slashed inside the joint (tips removed and reserved for another use)

1 cup ketchup

¼ cup mustard

¼ cup hot sauce

¼ cup soy sauce

1 tablespoon brown sugar

I call this my pantry sauce because you should have everything you need for it in your pantry.

• Yield: About 4 servings

Note: This recipe requires advance preparation.

The night before you plan to cook, cut the wings and put them in a zip bag. In a bowl, whisk together all the other ingredients and pour over the wings. Seal the bag and toss to coat.

Prepare the grill for direct cooking at medium heat. Put the wings directly on the grill, reserving the marinade in a bowl. Grill the wings, flipping occasionally and brushing with the marinade. Continue the flipping until the marinade is gone and the wings are browned and crispy. This should take about 30 minutes. The marinade should not be applied during the last 5 minutes of cooking, and if any is left it should be discarded.

Remove the wings to a platter and serve.

Rib Meat Potato Skins

6 large russet potatoes

2 cups coarsely chopped rib meat

2 cups shredded cheddar cheese

4 scallions, sliced

This is a great recipe for leftover barbecued ribs. I must admit that I rarely have any leftover rib meat, though, so I usually cook an extra slab and hide it so I can make these. • **Yield: 6 to 12 servings**

Preheat the oven to 350°F. Scrub the potatoes well and bake for about 1 hour. Cool the potatoes for at least 2 hours.

Prepare the grill for indirect cooking at 350°F, or preheat the oven to 350°F.

Cut the potatoes in half lengthwise. Spoon out most of the potato flesh and save for another use. (Home-fried potatoes?)

Place the skins on a baking sheet. Spoon the rib meat into the potato shells, distributing it evenly. Repeat the process with the cheese.

Cook until hot, bubbly, and browned, about 30 minutes. Top with chopped scallions and serve.

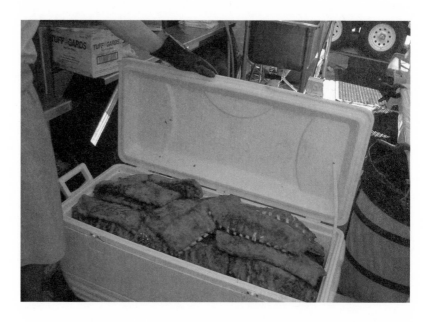

Gyro Meatballs

1 pound ground pork
(shoulder is best)

1 pound ground lamb
(shoulder is best)

1 egg, lightly beaten

¼ cup minced onion

3 cloves garlic, crushed

2 teaspoons dried oregano

1 teaspoon salt

1 teaspoon finely ground
black pepper

Juice of ½ lemon

¼ cup breadcrumbs

Pita bread, cut in wedges

Tzatziki Sauce (page 295)

If you ever find yourself heading west from Chicago on I-290, be sure to get off at Harlem Avenue and head to Kings N Queens for an authentic gyro sandwich. I've been eating there for thirty years and the food remains the same. In all those years I don't think they have ever messed up my order, either. It can be done. This is my barbecued attempt at re-creating that real taste of gyros at home. It's not really possible without that vertical spit that they use at Kings N Queens, but these little meatballs are pretty good.

• **Yield: About 50 meatballs**

Prepare the cooker for indirect cooking at 300°F, using apple wood for flavor.

In a large bowl, mix together the pork and the lamb. Add the egg and keep mixing. I have an old basic potato masher that I use for this. Add the onion, garlic, oregano, salt, pepper, and lemon juice and mix until it's all blended well. Add the breadcrumbs, half at a time, and keep mixing. As it comes together you'll probably have to use your hands. Form the mixture into little cocktail-size meatballs (about 1½ inches) and put them on a baking sheet. You should get about 50 meatballs.

There are a couple ways you can get them in and out of the cooker. I have a baking sheet that I have sacrificed to the smoke, so I just put them right on it in the cooker. You could transfer each meatball to the cooking grate, or you could get one of those cool black-coated grill grids with the holes in it. Put them on there and set it directly on the grate. Cook until the internal temp of the meatballs is about 150°F. This should take about 35 minutes.

Serve with wedges of pita bread and Tzatziki Sauce for dipping.

Queso Q'dido

2 tablespoons olive oil

2 links chorizo, removed from casing

2 poblano chiles, roasted, seeded, peeled, and chopped

2 jalapeño chiles, roasted, seeded, peeled, and chopped

3 cloves garlic, crushed

24 ounces Chihuahua cheese, grated (or jack cheese)

1 bunch green onions, sliced

Tortilla chips for serving

Barbecued cheese? *Sí!*
• Yield: 8 to 10 servings

Prepare the cooker for indirect cooking at 300°F, using cherry wood for flavor.

In a skillet on the stove, heat the oil and add the chorizo, cooking and breaking it into small pieces. Add the chiles and garlic and continue cooking until everything is soft. Transfer to a big bowl.

Add the cheese and green onions and toss to mix well. Transfer to a foil pan and place in the cooker. Heat until everything is hot and bubbly. This should take about 30 minutes.

Serve with tortilla chips.

Alfredo Lasagna with Smoked Chicken

2 large eggs, lightly beaten

One 15-ounce container ricotta cheese

1 teaspoon dried basil

3 cups shredded pepper jack cheese, divided

Two 16-ounce jars store-bought Alfredo sauce

One 9-ounce box "no boil" lasagna

4 cups coarsely chopped smoked chicken

Aside from all the appetizers at my Super Bowl party, there also needs to be a main course. Everybody wants to watch the game though, so I find that lasagna works out great. As long as we're talking barbecue here, let's make it a lasagna with smoked chicken. You can assemble it early in the day, or even the night before, cover, and refrigerate. Then just put it in the oven and it will be ready for your dinner. If it's been refrigerated, I like to let it sit at room temp for a half hour before it goes in the oven.

• **Yield: 8 to 10 servings**

Preheat the oven to 350°F.

In a medium bowl, mix together the eggs, ricotta, basil, and 2 cups of the pepper jack cheese.

Grease the bottom and sides of a 13 × 9-inch baking pan. Pour in about ¼ cup of Alfredo sauce and spread around the bottom. Lay four pieces of the lasagna in the bottom of the pan. Then put one-third of the chicken, one-third of the ricotta mixture, and one-third of 1 bottle of the sauce on top of the lasagna and spread it around.

Repeat this process 2 more times.

Top with the other jar of the sauce, spreading it around the sides. Top the whole thing with the last cup of cheese. Put in the oven and cook about 45 minutes or until browned and bubbly.

Let the whole pan rest for 10 minutes before serving.

Super Garlic Bread

2 sticks butter, softened

¼ cup freshly grated Parmesan cheese

1 tablespoon garlic powder

1 tablespoon paprika

1 teaspoon finely ground black pepper

2 thin soft loaves French bread

I learned to make garlic bread this way from my oldest and best friend, Mike Rice. Mike and I hung out together from about third grade until I moved away some thirty-five years later. We don't see each other much these days. He has a normal family life in suburban Chicago, and my life is, well, it's a little different than that. Mike is a really good cook. So is his mother, so I'd bet this came from her. You can assemble this early in the day, too, then just heat it with the lasagna. • **Yield: 8 to 10 servings**

Preheat the oven or the cooker to 350°F.

In a bowl, mix all the ingredients except the bread.

Make a series of cuts in each loaf, about 1½ inches apart, on an angle but not all the way through the bottom of the loaf. Spread both sides of each slice with a little bit of the butter mixture. Wrap the loaf in foil tightly. Repeat for the second loaf.

Put both loaves on the grill, or on a baking sheet in the oven. Cook for about 20 minutes for soft bread, and 30 minutes for crunchy bread.

Carnival:
Party-Time Outdoor Cooking

▼▼

The word "carnival" comes from the Latin *carne vale*, which means "farewell to meat." Carnival, also known as Mardi Gras, is the last hurrah before Ash Wednesday, and the beginning of Lent, when Christians are supposed to fast.

The most famous and festive carnivals are Mardi Gras in New Orleans, Carnival in Port of Spain, Trinidad, and Carnival in Rio de Janeiro, Brazil. All three involve masquerades, parades, drinking, and general partying down. This may surprise you but I've never been to Trinidad or Rio de Janeiro. I have been to New Orleans, though. I spent a week there one night. The food of New Orleans is spectacular. I don't generally go to the high-profile places; I much prefer to wander the French Quarter, stopping when

and where I please. I've rarely been disappointed. I even like an occasional Lucky Dog from the street vendors. My favorite bar in New Orleans is the Funky Pirate. They feature insane drinks like the Tropical Itch and the Shark Attack. They have pretty waitresses and the sounds of Big Al and the Blues Masters. I also enjoy the outdoor garden at Pat O'Brien's, home of the legendary rum-filled drink the Hurricane. This is a place where seemingly normal people stop for a Hurricane so they can get the souvenir glass, and they leave looking as if they've been drinking Hurricanes on Bourbon Street. It's a look you won't forget.

The last party-down day of Mardi Gras is also known as Fat Tuesday. I'm proud to offer up a barbecue menu for that day.

Dr. BBQ's Barbecued Barbecue Shrimp

Dr. BBQ's Carnival in Your Mouth Gumbo

King's Cake

▼▼▼▼▼

Dr. BBQ's Barbecued Barbecue Shrimp

2 sticks butter

2 bay leaves

3 cloves garlic, crushed

1 teaspoon dried thyme

1 teaspoon dried oregano

1 teaspoon dried basil

1 tablespoon coarsely ground black pepper

1 tablespoon paprika

1 tablespoon Louisiana hot sauce

¼ cup Worcestershire sauce

Juice of 1 lemon

½ cup beer

Bamboo skewers soaked in water for at least 1 hour

2 pounds jumbo shrimp, peeled and deveined

2 teaspoons Dr. BBQ's Creole Seasoning (page 283)

That name is a mouthful, and so is this shrimp dish. Pascal's Manale Restaurant in New Orleans is credited with creating a famous dish they call barbecue shrimp. These shrimp don't seem to have any possible tie to actual barbecue, though, as they are cooked in a pan on the stove. I've seen pork and beef that was cooked in the oven and served with a traditional barbecue sauce, but these are served in a sauce made with butter, garlic, herbs, Creole seasoning, and Worcestershire sauce. They're really good, and nobody seems to care that they aren't really barbecued, so I don't either. My version doesn't include the heads or shells. That's kind of a Gulf Coast thing. My version does get grilled for a couple of minutes, just to add a little flavor. That's why I call them Barbecued Barbecue Shrimp. • **Yield: 6 to 8 servings as an appetizer**

Prepare the grill for direct cooking at medium high heat, using pecan wood for flavor.

In a large skillet on the stove, melt the butter over medium heat. Add all the other ingredients except the skewers, shrimp, and the Creole seasoning. Bring to a simmer and cook, stirring occasionally, for about 5 minutes. Remove from the heat.

Skewer the shrimp with double skewers so they can be flipped easily. Season the shrimp with Dr. BBQ's Creole Seasoning. Grill for about 1 minute per side. Remove from the heat and then remove from the skewers.

Add the shrimp to the pan with the butter mixture and toss. Let rest 5 minutes. Return to the stove over medium-high heat and bring to a simmer.

Check the shrimp for doneness by breaking 1, and check for salt, adding some if necessary. Turn the heat off and remove the shrimp to a bowl, using a slotted spoon. Pour the sauce over the top.

Serve with lots of crusty bread for sopping up the sauce.

Dr. BBQ's Carnival in Your Mouth Gumbo

I'm not sure where I learned how to make gumbo—probably a combination of reading books on Louisiana cooking, watching Justin Wilson, and stumbling around New Orleans. I guess the truth is I have never really learned because I don't think I make mine in a very traditional fashion. But I do think the outcome is pretty much on the money. I don't add okra or filé, mainly because I don't care for either of them. Feel free to add them if you like. Good gumbo is so full of flavors that nothing should stand out. I resist the obvious temptation to use smoked chicken in my gumbo, as I like to use the chicken to make a stock to be used in the gumbo. You can cook the poor chicken only so many times. I use store-bought smoked sausage but by all means use some you've smoked yourself if you have it. I am certainly not Cajun, but I am primarily of French descent. My people came through Ellis Island and went directly to a bastion of French immigrants in southern Illinois. If they had come a little earlier and headed to Nova Scotia, well, who knows? The truth is that smothered dishes that are so much a part of the cuisine of south Louisiana are very much like what my grandma Julia Hameau used to cook for us when I was growing up. I still cook that way often. She made pan gravies out of almost everything she cooked and often used tomato sauce to finish a sauce as a classic French chef would use cream and butter. I tend to think of hers as

The Stock

2 quarts water

8 chicken thighs

2 carrots, peeled

3 ribs celery, washed

1 medium onion, peeled and quartered

3 cloves garlic, sliced

2 vegetable bouillon cubes (or chicken will work fine)

1 teaspoon salt

1 tablespoon coarsely ground black pepper

The Roux

¾ cup corn oil

¾ cup all-purpose flour

The Gumbo

2 cups chopped onion

2 cups chopped celery

2 cups chopped green bell pepper

6 cloves garlic, crushed

1 pound smoked sausage, halved and sliced

2 or 3 jalapeños, chopped, seeds included

One 28-ounce can diced tomatoes

1 tablespoon salt

the peasant version. My grandfather was a coal miner, so they sure weren't living the high life.

This dish isn't grilled or smoked, but making gumbo is a lot like cooking barbecue. It's an all-day affair at my house. Sometimes even a two-day affair, since the gumbo is even better reheated. I like to make a pot early in the week and reheat it Friday night at a cookoff. I do insist on fresh rice, though. I carry my rice cooker with me everywhere. It's a no-brainer to use and makes perfect rice every time.

• Yield: About 12 servings, or 2 Cajuns

(That's an old Justin Wilson joke.)

Note: This recipe requires advance preparation.

At least 8 hours before you plan to eat, or preferably the day before, heat the water in a large Dutch oven. As the water heats add the other stock ingredients and bring to a boil. Immediately reduce to a simmer. Cover and cook for 1 hour. Remove from the heat and let the mixture rest for another hour. Pour the mixture through a colander. Reserve the liquid. Reserve the vegetables for another use, or have them for a snack. Let the chicken cool and remove the skin and bones, keeping the chicken in large pieces. If you're making this a day ahead, the chicken and stock must now be refrigerated.

Preheat a large Dutch oven over medium heat. Add the oil and flour. Cook, stirring constantly with a wooden spoon, until the roux is a dark brown chocolate color. This will take a long time and can't be rushed. I timed one recently and it took over an hour. Be very careful not to burn the roux or you'll need to start all over. Turn the heat down if you need to. This is particularly high risk toward the end. As soon as you think the roux is dark enough, or your nerve runs out,

1 tablespoon coarsely ground black pepper

1½ tablespoons dried thyme

8 cups cooked white rice

add the onion, celery, and green pepper and continue stirring. This will cool the roux and end the risk of it burning.

Continue stirring for about 5 minutes, until the vegetables get soft. Add the reserved chicken and the garlic, sausage, and jalapeños. Continue stirring for another 5 minutes. Add the canned tomatoes with their juice and cook another 5 minutes.

Add 2 quarts of the stock and the salt, pepper, and thyme. Bring to a boil, reduce the heat, and simmer on low for 2 hours, adding more stock as needed. If the stock runs out just add water. When done, the consistency should be a thick soup.

Check for salt and serve in bowls with the rice piled along the side.

King's Cake

The Dough

½ cup lukewarm water

2 packages dry yeast

5 cups sifted all-purpose flour

½ cup sugar

½ teaspoon freshly grated nutmeg

2 teaspoons salt

1 teaspoon grated lemon zest

½ cup lukewarm milk

3 eggs

4 egg yolks

½ cup plus 2 tablespoons softened butter

1 dried kidney bean

1 egg, lightly beaten with 1 tablespoon milk

The Sugars

Green, purple, and yellow food coloring pastes (not liquid)

12 tablespoons sugar

The Icing

3 cups confectioner's sugar

¼ cup strained, freshly squeezed lemon juice

3 to 6 tablespoons water

The tradition of baking a special cake at Christmastime with a bean inside originated in Europe to honor the three kings who visited the baby Jesus. The person who was served the piece of cake with the bean in it traditionally played the role of one of the kings. Louisianians, always looking for fun, extended the tradition through the season to Mardi Gras, and the person finding the bean was required to throw another party and bake another king's cake. The Louisiana king's cake is decorated with bright-colored sugars in the Mardi Gras colors of green, purple, and gold. • **Yield: 8 servings**

To make the dough, combine the water and yeast in a bowl and mix well.

In another bowl, combine the flour, sugar, nutmeg, salt, and lemon zest and mix. In the center of the flour mixture, make a well and pour the yeast mixture and milk into it.

Add the eggs and egg yolks, and with a large wooden spoon, gradually incorporate the dry ingredients into the liquid ones. Beat in the ½ cup butter and continue beating until a dough ball forms. (This can also be done in a food processor.) Place the dough ball on a floured board and knead until the dough is smooth and elastic, adding more flour if necessary.

Brush the inside of a large bowl with 1 tablespoon of the softened butter. Place the dough ball in the bowl and coat it with butter. Cover the bowl and let sit for 1½ hours or until it doubles in size.

Brush a large baking sheet with the remaining butter. Preheat the oven to 375°F. Remove the dough to a lightly floured surface and punch it down. Knead it and then shape it into a cylinder about 14 inches long. Place on the baking sheet and form it into a ring. Press the bean into the dough so that it is hidden. Brush the dough all over with the egg-milk mixture and bake for 25 to 30 minutes, until golden brown. Remove and place on a wire rack to cool.

To make the sugars, squeeze a bit of the green paste into the palm of one hand. Sprinkle 2 tablespoons of sugar over the paste and rub your hands together to coat the sugar granules. Transfer each sugar to a bowl until needed. Make 4 tablespoons of each color and do not mix the sugars.

To prepare the icing, combine the confectioner's sugar, lemon juice, and 3 tablespoons of water in a deep bowl and stir until smooth. If too stiff to spread, add more water, 1 teaspoon at a time, and continue stirring.

With a flexible knife or spatula, spread the icing over the top of the cake, allowing it to run down the sides. Sprinkle the colored sugars over the icing, forming a row of purple, yellow, and green strips, each about 2 inches wide, on both sides of the ring.

Valentine's Day:
The Romantic Grill

▼▼

H.E. Wedeck, the author of *Dictionary of Aphrodisiacs*, writes, "The oyster does not seem to deserve its reputation as an aphrodisiac," but I still don't care. Smoked oysters are delicious and they have, you know, a reputation. So do shrimp, scallops, and most seafood, so they're on the menu, too. Lamb is not included in Wedeck's dictionary even though I learned that, in ancient Persia, lamb's feet "steeped in vinegar as a love enticement" were presented to newly married couples. I'm not going to make those, though. I'm making rack of lamb.

I think it's interesting that we celebrate Valentine's Day on the day that Saint Valentine was *beheaded*. He was a Roman priest who secretly married couples in defiance of Emperor Claudius the Cruel, who didn't allow marriage. He got caught, lost his head, and eventually was made a saint. Saint Valentine is also the patron saint of beekeepers, engaged couples, epilepsy, fainting, plague, travelers, and young people, so he really gets around. Now we make a big deal over his day, and a lot of money is spent on expensive gifts that somehow prove our love.

Chocolate candies are a common Valentine gift, of course, and have their own reputation as an aphrodisiac. I'm going to give a box of those, but I'm adding a chocolate mousse for dessert.

Cupid's Smoked Oysters

Dizzy Rack of Lamb

Grilled Balsamic Eggplant

**Twice-Baked Sweet Potatoes
with Honey Cinnamon Butter**

Dark Chocolate Mousse with a Hint of Red Chile

▼▼▼▼▼

Cupid's Smoked Oysters

¼ **cup dry vermouth**

2 tablespoons chopped shallots

1½ sticks cold butter

Grated lemon zest

Salt and freshly ground black pepper to taste

Rock salt

24 unshucked oysters, scrubbed and rinsed

Lemon wedges

I could eat all twenty-four of these babies myself! They are only lightly smoked, so the oyster flavor shines through. This recipe brings to mind the time a satisfied lover said to me, "Do you smoke after making love?" I answered, "I don't know, I never looked." • **Yield: 4 servings**

Prepare the grill for direct grilling at high heat, using apple wood for flavor.

Combine the vermouth and shallots in a saucepan and cook until only 1 tablespoon of liquid is left. Reduce the heat to very low. Cut the butter into small slices and whisk 1 piece at a time into the reduced liquid until the sauce is thick. Add the lemon zest and salt and pepper and keep the sauce warm.

Add rock salt to a large, shallow pan and heat in the oven. Place the oysters, flat side up, directly on the hot grill and close the top of the grill. Check every 5 minutes and when the oysters have opened, remove them from the grill.

Wearing heavy gloves, shuck the oysters and place them in their shells in the rock salt to keep warm. Drizzle a little sauce over each oyster and serve them with the lemon wedges.

Dizzy Rack of Lamb

A Recipe from Barbecue All Star Chris Capell

2 Frenched racks of lamb

2 tablespoons olive oil, or enough to coat very lightly

The Rub (makes about ⅔ cup)

2 tablespoons whole black peppercorns

½ tablespoon whole coriander seeds

3 tablespoons coarse kosher or sea salt

2 tablespoons turbinado sugar

1 tablespoon granulated onion

1 tablespoon granulated garlic

1 tablespoon finely ground coffee

1 tablespoon mild ground chiles (ancho, New Mexico, and/or Chimayo)

1 teaspoon ground cumin

½ teaspoon chipotle chile powder

Chris Capell is a guy I met through the Big Green Egg users' forum on the Internet. His handle is Nature Boy, based on his interest in remote camping. He even camps during the dead of winter. I won't be doing any of that with him, but we do share a passion for cooking good food. Chris is a talented artist, too, but his current profession is making and selling spice blends. He's passionate about freshness and getting specific, high-quality ingredients, and it shows in his products. Chris has also gotten some friends together to compete in some cookoffs, and they've done very well. The whole story, along with a place to order his stuff, is at www.dizzypigbbq.com, but you can't buy the spice in this recipe. He made this one just for my book, and I truly appreciate it. One interesting note: This recipe contains no herbs, which is pretty radical for a lamb recipe, but it works well.

Chris's words. "I tried my first rack of lamb a few years ago after noticing that another team had entered one in the miscellaneous category at a barbecue competition. Not only did I love it, but so did the judges who voted it first place. Since then I have cooked a bunch of racks and have found some interesting flavors that work well with this wonderful cut. The simplicity of the preparation is not obvious when you serve this impressive dish . . . yet a good rub and a hot fire is all you need."

- **Yield: 4 servings**

Rub the lamb racks lightly with a thin coat of olive oil. Grind the peppercorns and coriander in a small coffee grinder, food processor, or with a mortar and pestle. Mix these together with all of the other rub ingredients and, if possible, pulse a few times in a small food processor. Coat the lamb generously with the rub and press into the meat. Let rub melt in for 30 minutes to 4 hours.

Prepare the grill for direct cooking at high heat.

On a clean grate, directly over a very hot fire, carefully sear the meat side of the lamb for 1 to 3 minutes, or until lightly charred (watch closely to prevent sugar from burning). Flip and sear on the other side. Once you have the desired color and char reduce heat and place lamb so it is not directly over the fire. Cook at 300 to 400°F until the meat reaches 130 to 135°F internal temperature, about 20 minutes, depending on the temp and size of rack.

Rest the meat on a plate for 10 to 15 minutes. Slice between the bones. Dredge the "chops" through the juice on the plate and serve.

Grilled Balsamic Eggplant

2 small eggplants, peeled and cut in half lengthwise

¼ cup olive oil

1 tablespoon balsamic vinegar

1 clove garlic, crushed

½ teaspoon salt

½ teaspoon dried oregano

½ teaspoon coarsely ground black pepper

Here's a twist on grilled veggies using eggplant. If you can find those little Japanese eggplants, just grill one for each guest as a side dish. • **Yield: 4 servings**

Note: This recipe requires advance preparation.

The night before you plan to cook, salt the eggplants and allow them to drain in a colander for about 1 hour to take away the bitterness. Rinse the salt off and pat dry with paper towels.

Whisk all the rest of the ingredients together in a bowl. Put the eggplants in a zip bag and pour the marinade over them. Seal the bag and toss to coat evenly.

Prepare the grill for direct cooking at high heat. Remove the eggplants from the marinade. Place directly on the grill. Cook about 5 minutes until brown. Flip and cook another 5 minutes. The eggplant should be fork tender.

Remove from the grill and slice into bite-size pieces. Check for salt and add if needed.

Twice-Baked Sweet Potatoes with Honey Cinnamon Butter

2 medium sweet potatoes, rinsed and dried

¾ cup softened butter

½ cup honey

1 teaspoon ground cinnamon, or more to taste

They say sweets for the sweet, so this dish should turn everyone on! • **Yield: 4 servings**

Bake the sweet potatoes in a 400°F oven until they are easily pierced with a knife, about 1 hour. Remove them from the oven, cut them in half lengthwise, and, using gloves and a spoon, remove all the sweet potato from the skin into a bowl. Reserve the skins.

Add the butter, honey, and cinnamon to the bowl and mix well. Return the mixture to the skins, place them on a baking sheet, and return them to the oven for 20 minutes.

Dark Chocolate Mousse
with a Hint of Red Chile

1 teaspoon butter

4 ounces semisweet chocolate

2 ounces unsweetened baker's chocolate

7 tablespoons lemon liqueur

1 teaspoon New Mexican red chile powder

5 eggs, separated

Lemon slices for garnish

Both chocolate and chiles are reputed aphrodisiacs, so why not combine them as the Aztecs did?

• **Yield: 4 servings**

Lightly butter a saucepan, place it over low heat, and add the 2 chocolates. As the chocolate starts to melt, add 5 tablespoons of the lemon liqueur and the chile powder.

When the chocolate is completely melted, add the egg yolks, 1 at a time, mixing well after each addition. Remove from heat and add the remaining 2 tablespoons of lemon liqueur. Mix gently.

Beat the egg whites until they form soft peaks and fold them thoroughly into the chocolate mixture. Pour into a 2-quart soufflé dish and refrigerate for at least 2 hours.

Serve garnished with the lemon slices.

The Daytona 500:
Race Day Barbecue

▼▼

The opening of the NASCAR season is a perfect excuse for a barbecue. It all began when the Land Speed Records runs actually had cars racing on the packed sands of Daytona Beach. In 1936 stock car racing began on a track that was half on the beach and half on city streets. It was a 3.2-mile course. Finally, in 1959, Daytona International Speedway began operation after being built at a cost of $3 million, which doesn't seem like all that much money now. Today, the speedway is the largest sporting arena in the Southeast, covering 480 acres and seating more that 165,000 race fans. Did you know that the Daytona 500 is the biggest motor sports event in the country, surpassing even the Indianapolis 500? It has the most total prize money, the largest attendance, and the biggest TV audience. The Daytona 500 is also considered to be the "Super Bowl" of NASCAR, yet they start the season with it.

When I lived in Chicago I didn't know much about stock car racing, but since moving to the South I have been shown the way. It's the perfect Sunday afternoon sport for TV. I usually watch the beginning of the race, as it's very exciting and orients you to the issues that will be in play on that day. Then you are free to nap as you need to. You may miss an occasional pit stop or a breakdown of your favorite driver, but the announcers will get you caught up when you wake up. Then you'll need to be awake for the last hour or so, because that's when it gets really exciting. It's amazing how many women are big NASCAR fans, too. My friend Robin Tibbetts is a very intelligent, normal, grown woman with an 8 tattooed on her leg because she is a fan of Dale Earnhardt, Jr. I must admit that I am a fan of the 8, too, but I have resisted the tattoo.

What to serve on Daytona 500 day? It's a big day so I say spring for some ribs. It's also a good day to drink some cold beer, so I'm going to spice the food up a little.

Pit Stop Chicken Wings

Race Day Ribs

Spiced-Up Potato Salad

Dr. BBQ's Sweet Cream Corn

Checkered Flag Cake

▼▼▼▼

Pit Stop Chicken Wings

12 whole chicken wings, slashed inside the joint (tips removed and reserved for another use)

Dr. BBQ's Bonesmokers Crank It Up! Pepper Blend*

Orange-Honey Glaze (page 299)

*Dr. BBQ's Bonesmokers Crank It Up! Pepper Blend is a commercial product that is available through my Web site, www.drbbq.com. If you don't have any you can substitute a blend of dried ground peppers and chiles that you have available.

Yield: 4 to 6 servings

Prepare the grill for direct cooking at medium heat.

Season the wings liberally with Dr. BBQ's Bonesmokers Crank It Up! Pepper Blend. Put the wings directly on the grill. Cook the wings, flipping them occasionally, until they start to brown and are close to being done.

Begin brushing with the Orange-Honey Glaze.

Continue flipping and brushing until the wings are cooked and nicely browned. This should take about 30 minutes total.

Remove to a plate and serve.

Race Day Ribs

2 slabs spare ribs, about 4 pounds each

Peggy's Favorite Barbecue Rub (page 278)

½ cup apple juice, divided

Dr. BBQ's Race Day Barbecue Sauce (page 285)

These are traditional barbecued spare ribs with a spicy barbecue sauce. Be sure to cut through each rib before serving. Let's go racing! • **Yield: 4 servings**

Prepare the cooker for indirect cooking at 275°F, using two parts cherry wood and one part hickory wood for flavor.

Peel the membrane off the back of the ribs. Season the ribs liberally with the rub. Place the ribs in the cooker, meaty side up. Cook for about 3 hours, or until the ribs have a nice brown color and are beginning to get soft. Remove the ribs from the cooker.

Lay out a big double layer of foil for each slab. Lay the ribs on the foil, meaty side up. As you begin to close up the foil into a package around the ribs, add half the apple juice to each packet. Now wrap the ribs up tightly, being careful not to puncture the foil.

Put the ribs back in the cooker for another 1½ hours, or until they reach your desired degree of tenderness.

Take the ribs out of the foil but leave them on the cooker. Brush both sides with some of the barbecue sauce and cook for another 20 minutes.

Remove the ribs to a platter and let them rest for 5 minutes. Lay each slab on a cutting board, meat side down, and cut through the slab to separate every rib. Transfer them to a platter and serve with barbecue sauce on the side.

Spiced-Up Potato Salad

4 medium russet potatoes

¼ cup olive oil

¼ cup white wine vinegar

2½ teaspoons red New Mexican chile powder

1 teaspoon bottled hot sauce

½ cup chopped onion

One 8-ounce can whole kernel corn, drained and rinsed

½ cup coarsely shredded carrot

⅓ cup chopped green bell pepper

½ cup sliced ripe olives (optional)

This is an unusual—but very tasty—potato salad. It is very easy to adjust the heat level, so you might want to make it with half the chile powder and then add more at the end if it's not spicy enough for you.

• **Yield: 4 to 6 servings**

Place the potatoes in a large Dutch-style casserole and cover with water. Bring the water to a boil and turn the heat down so the water is at a gentle boil. Cook for 15 to 20 minutes, or until a knife pierces the potatoes easily. Drain, peel, and cube them into a large bowl while still warm.

In a small glass jar, combine the oil, vinegar, chile powder, and hot sauce and shake vigorously. Pour over the potatoes and toss gently. Add the remaining ingredients and toss gently.

Refrigerate for 1 hour before serving.

Dr. BBQ's Sweet Cream Corn

½ stick butter

2 pounds frozen corn kernels

One 3-ounce block cream cheese, cut into cubes

1 cup heavy cream

1 tablespoon sugar

½ teaspoon salt

1 teaspoon coarsely ground black pepper

I had some really great creamed corn at a barbecue joint in Albuquerque, so I decided to make my own version. I think it's a great barbecue side dish. • **Yield: 8 servings**

In a large saucepan over low heat, add the butter and then the corn. Add the cream cheese on top and cover. Stir occasionally until the corn is defrosted and the cream cheese begins to melt.

Add the heavy cream, sugar, salt, and pepper and continue cooking, raising the heat to medium and stirring occasionally.

Bring to a simmer and cook for 5 minutes.

Checkered Flag Cake

The Cake

2½ cups sifted all-purpose flour

¼ cup cocoa

1 teaspoon baking soda

1 teaspoon salt

½ cup butter

½ cup vegetable oil

1¾ cups sugar

2 eggs

1 teaspoon vanilla

¾ to 1 cup buttermilk

The White Icing

2 cups sifted confectioner's sugar

¼ cup soft butter

½ cup milk, or more to adjust consistency

1 teaspoon vanilla

The Dark Icing

3 ounces semisweet chocolate

2 tablespoons butter

2¾ cups sifted confectioner's sugar

½ teaspoon salt

1 teaspoon vanilla

6 tablespoons light cream, or more to adjust consistency

I know it sounds like Janet from Party Planners of Lakeland gave me this recipe, but I swear she didn't. It all came to me in a dream while I was napping during the Daytona 500. • **Yield: 8 to 10 servings**

Preheat the oven to 325°F.

Sift together the flour, cocoa, baking soda, and salt in a large mixing bowl. Set aside.

In a separate bowl, cream the butter, vegetable oil, and sugar. Beat with an electric mixer until the mixture is light and fluffy. Beat in the eggs 1 at a time. Next, add the vanilla.

Mix in the dry ingredients, alternating with the buttermilk. The batter should be medium-thick. Pour into a greased 13 × 9 × 2-inch pan. Bake the cake for about 55 minutes. Cool the pan on a wire rack.

While the cake is baking, make the icings. To make the white icing, combine all the ingredients in a bowl and mix until the consistency is thin enough to apply with a pastry bag. To make the dark icing, melt the chocolate and the butter in a double boiler over hot water. Add the remaining ingredients and mix well for 10 minutes. The consistency should be thin enough to apply with a pastry bag.

Pour the white icing into a pastry bag. Using a ruler as a guide, make a grid pattern on top of the cake. Fill in every other square with the white icing. Using another pastry bag, fill it with the dark icing and fill in the remaining squares to make the flag.

Spring

A New Barbecue Beginning

Saint Patrick's Day:
Can You Believe Dublin Barbecue?

March Madness:
Hooped-Up 'Cue

April Fool's Day:
Faux Food Follies

Tax Day:
Hard Times Barbecue

Earth Day:
Salt of the Earth Barbecue

Easter:
A Family Barbecue Feast

May Day:
Another Excuse to Barbecue

A Springtime Picnic:
Portable Grilling

Cinco de Mayo:
Southwestern 'Cue

Mother's Day:
Barbecue for Mom

▼▼▼▼▼

Since most of your grilling and smoking will be done in the next three seasons, it makes sense to get a fresh start in the spring. First, extend the concept of spring cleaning to your grills and smoker and get rid of the winter grit. Take the cooking grates off, place them in a plastic bag, and spray them with oven cleaner. Let them marinate overnight and then just rinse them off with the hose. Treat any grease on your units with a spray cleaner, then use soapy water. Just be sure to rinse everything well before cooking.

It's also time to stock up on supplies, so buy charcoal, various wood or wood chips, fire starters, and fresh spices. You can usually find freshly stocked shelves at the stores, with some new items and even spring sales during the month of May. If you use propane, buy an extra canister and keep it filled—then you won't feel like an idiot when you run out of gas in the middle of grilling that chicken. Spring is also a good time to consider upgrading your cookers, or just adding a new one. If one grill is good, then three must be better. In my biased opinion, at least one grill and one smoker should be on every deck.

Every year brings new things from all the grill companies. With the popularity boom of barbecuing, they are really trying to outdo each other now. Be sure to look around before buying a new grill, because you never know what will be next. I like the gas grills with three burners left to right. That way I can light the two outside burners and cook indirect in the middle. I also like the cast-iron grids, and an infrared back burner for the rotisserie is a must. Beyond that there are lights and drawers and smoke boxes and warmers and big, beautiful stainless steel cabinets. Your credit card is about the only limit to what you can get.

I've also seen a new breed of fancy heavy-duty charcoal grills coming to the market. I think this is just great. Cooking with charcoal just isn't as much of a hassle as some folks want to make it out to be, and the taste is unmatched. These things are big and black and cool-looking. I'm sure they all work well direct and indirect, and you should be able to use natural lump charcoal. Speaking of natural lump charcoal, that's what you have to use in the Big Green Egg. They have a new 24-inch grid model they are calling the XL. You could cook three turkeys on it with room for some other dishes in between. It's no secret that I like the Egg, and they continue to impress me all the time.

The other new trend I've seen is in high-quality portable grills. There are some great little fold-up portable gas grills. These things can double as the home grill too, if you don't have a big family. My friend Dave DeWitt has a little tiny, miserly charcoal grill called the Cobb. He can cook a great chicken on it in ninety minutes with six briquettes. That's amazing! Then there's that fold-up one they are always using at the beach in the commercial. It looks pretty good, too.

Obviously these small grills are all great for tailgating, but there is also a series of larger grills that will hook right into your trailer hitch and ride right behind you kind of like a bike rack. These are nice because you don't have to worry about getting it all cooled down and cleaned up to go back in the SUV for the ride home. I would make sure the fire is out, though. Some are even part of a portable kitchen, with a CD player and a little refrigerator.

Smokers are also getting to be very available in the mainstream. It's just not that long ago that you couldn't buy a true smoker in the Northern states. Now they are everywhere. I just saw a really nice-looking stainless steel propane-fueled smoker at one of the big club stores. It would look great right next to any fancy gas grill. Weber makes a great "bullet"-type water smoker for under $200, and there are similar configurations even cheaper. Of course there are great big fancy ones, too. Any guy wants one of these. My Cookshack FEC100 is as good as it gets in any size or shape and it'll fit nicely in any backyard.

If you just aren't in the market for a new grill this year, shine yours up, get it some new parts, and get cooking. Spring is here!

Saint Patrick's Day:
Can You Believe Dublin Barbecue?

▼▼

I hate to smash your shamrock, but Saint Patrick's given name was not Patrick (it was probably Maewyn), he was not born in Ireland, and we celebrate the date of his death, not his birth. As far as we know, Saint Patrick was born in Britain to wealthy parents near the end of the fourth century. He is believed to have died on March 17, around A.D. 460. Although his father was a Christian deacon, it has been suggested that he probably took on the role because of tax incentives, and there is no evidence that Patrick came from a particularly religious family. At the age of sixteen, Patrick was taken prisoner by a group of Irish raiders who were attacking his family's estate. They transported him to Ireland, where he spent six years in captivity. During this time, he worked as a shepherd, outdoors and away from people. He turned to his religion for solace, becoming a devout Christian. Saint Patrick is now hailed as the patron saint of Ireland, shamrocks, and harps. Not much is known about his style of cooking, but since he lived in the fifth century, you can bet that the heat source was wood or peat.

These days we make a big deal of celebrating all things Irish with parades, the wearing of the green, and the conspicuous consumption of green beer and corned beef and cabbage, and by listening to Irish music. Not me. I have to cook, but I will take a moment or two to toast Saint Patrick with a wee toddy of good Irish whiskey while I'm standing at the smoker.

To smash another myth, corned beef and cabbage is not an authentic Irish dish—the early Irish raised cows for their milk, and their favorite meat was pork. Cows were simply too valuable to eat—except by kings, whose cooks preserved the beef by "corning" it, which involved curing it by rolling it in large crystals ("corns") of salt. But Irish immigrants to Canada and the United States in the nineteenth century found cheap beef and cheap salt to corn it in the Irish method, and the dish became so popular in the West that even Irish restaurants in Ireland serve it today—to tourists. They don't cook it in the smoker, but I sure do.

Green Beer

New World Smoked Corned Beef

Shamrock Potatoes

Grilled Cabbage and Onions with Beer

Irish Turnips and Carrots

Irish Mist Cheesecake

▼▼▼▼

Green Beer

1 pint Harp Lager, or your
favorite beer

A few drops of liquid
green food coloring

I can't imagine anything weirder that is so widely accepted. This could only happen on Saint Patrick's Day. It really doesn't do anything to the beer except make it look festive. • **Yield: 1 pint**

Put the food coloring in the beer and give it a quick stir.

New World Smoked Corned Beef

One 3- to 4-pound piece of corned beef, flat cut

Freshly ground black pepper to taste

Here's a new twist on an old favorite.
• Yield: 6 to 8 servings

Prepare the cooker to cook indirect at 275°F, using hickory and cherry wood for flavor.

Take the corned beef out of the package and sprinkle it with black pepper. Put it in the cooker and cook for 2 hours.

Take it off the cooker, wrap it in foil, and add ¼ cup of water before you seal the foil packet.

Put it back on the smoker and cook until it reaches an internal temp of 185°F. This should be about another 2 hours.

Remove from the cooker and let it rest for 20 minutes. Slice thinly.

Shamrock Potatoes

3 to 4 pounds red creamer new potatoes

1 stick butter

1 teaspoon dried parsley

1 teaspoon dried thyme

1 teaspoon dried marjoram

1 teaspoon coarsely ground black pepper

Salt to taste

These simple potatoes are a great accompaniment to any grilled dish. I like to leave just part of the skins on. It makes a nice presentation and the end result isn't overwhelmed by too much skin. It is a potato dish, after all.

• **Yield: 6 to 8 servings**

Prepare a kettle of boiling salted water. Peel the potatoes around the middle, leaving the skin on both ends. Put the potatoes in the boiling water and cook until fork tender, about 8 to 10 minutes.

Meanwhile, in a small saucepan melt the butter and add the herbs and pepper. Remove from the heat.

When the potatoes are done, drain them well and put them in a large bowl. Pour the melted butter mixture over them and toss to coat them all evenly.

Check for salt and add if needed.

Grilled Cabbage and Onions with Beer

1 medium head of
cabbage, quartered

1 medium onion, quartered

½ cup olive oil

1 tablespoon salt

1 tablespoon coarsely
ground black pepper

1 tablespoon sugar

1 can beer

You've never heard of grilled cabbage? Well, these days just about anything can be grilled.

• Yield: 6 to 8 servings

Prepare the grill for direct cooking at high heat. Brush the cabbage and onion quarters with the olive oil. Grill them until they are nicely browned; this should take about 20 minutes.

Preheat the oven to 350°F. Transfer the cabbage and onions to a baking pan. Sprinkle with the salt, pepper, and sugar. Pour the beer over the top. Cover tightly with foil and put in the oven. Cook for 30 minutes or until the cabbage and onions are soft.

Pour off most of the liquid and toss the cabbage and onion together, breaking them up. Check for salt. Transfer to a bowl and serve.

Irish Turnips and Carrots

2 medium turnips, peeled
and quartered

2 pounds carrots, peeled

1 parsnip, peeled

1 stick butter, softened

Salt and freshly ground
black pepper to taste

I grew up with lots of Irish friends around Chicago. My friend Ellen Rice always served this dish at holiday dinners. It's really good, and the ingredients all kind of go together, and it's just not something I've seen anywhere else.

• **Yield 8 to 10 servings**

Prepare a large kettle of boiling salted water. Put all the vegetables in and cook them until tender, about 20 minutes. Drain and transfer to a large bowl. Add the butter and some salt and pepper. Mash them all with a potato masher, leaving them kind of chunky. Check for salt and pepper and add if needed.

Irish Mist Cheesecake

The Crust

1⅓ cups chocolate wafer crumbs

¼ cup butter, softened

1 tablespoon sugar

The Filling

1½ cups semisweet chocolate pieces

¼ cup Irish Mist

2 tablespoons butter

2 eggs, beaten

⅓ cup sugar

¼ teaspoon salt

1 cup sour cream

Two 8-ounce packages cream cheese, softened and cut into pieces

Whipped cream and chocolate shavings for serving (optional)

Use that famous liqueur made from Irish whiskey to liven up this dessert. • **Yield: 10 servings**

Preheat the oven to 350°F.

To make the crust, in a small bowl mix together the wafer crumbs, butter, and sugar and press firmly in a 9-inch springform pan.

In a small saucepan, over medium heat, melt the chocolate with the Irish Mist and butter. Stir until smooth. Set aside.

In a medium bowl, combine the eggs, sugar, and salt. Add the sour cream and blend well. Add the cream cheese to the egg mixture and beat until smooth. Gradually blend in the chocolate mixture. Turn into the prepared crust and bake for 35 minutes or until the filling is barely set in the center.

Turn off the heat and let the cake stand in the oven for 15 minutes with the door open. Take it out of the oven and let it stand at room temperature for 1 hour.

Cover loosely and refrigerate for several hours or overnight. You can garnish it with whipped cream and chocolate shavings.

March Madness:
Hooped-Up 'Cue

▼▼▼

March Madness, aka the NCAA basketball tournament, is a good reason for a barbecue. For my basketball blowout, I almost called Janet of Party Planners of Lakeland, but then I thought about a centerpiece involving a freshly scrubbed basketball and spring lilies, so

I decided to go in another direction. I would smoke a huge, spherical hamburger the size of a basketball in my Big Green Egg. Hell, it would fit under the dome lid, and I could call it "Smoked Basketball Meat Loaf with Dribbled Sauce," or maybe not.

Air Ball Bloody Mary

Three-Point-Play Grilled Nachos

Full Court Press Grilled Pork Loin Salad

No-Foul Chicken Fajitas with Grilled Onion Guacamole

Slam-Dunk Dessert: Bread Pudding with Tequila Sauce

▼▼▼▼

Air Ball Bloody Mary

½ teaspoon of your favorite bottled hot sauce, or more to taste

1½ ounces fine vodka such as Stolichnaya or Absolut

3 ounces tomato juice, freshly made from vine-ripened tomatoes, or more to taste

1 teaspoon freshly squeezed lime juice

⅛ teaspoon soy sauce

1/16 teaspoon brown sugar

1 dash salt

Freshly ground black pepper to taste

Slice of serrano or jalapeño chile for garnish

Since the games start early on the weekend, you're going to need a bracer to get you going. Here it is, the ultimate Bloody Mary designed for the ultimate peppery cocktail snob. Canned tomato juice is permitted only when fresh, vine-ripened tomatoes are not available. Be sure to buy the ice cube trays that produce spherical cubes like miniature basketballs. • **Yield: 1 serving**

Combine all ingredients and shake with spherical ice cubes. Serve garnished with a slice of fresh serrano or jalapeño chile.

Three-Point-Play Grilled Nachos

12 corn tortillas, cut into triangles

Vegetable oil for frying

1 cup finely diced tomatoes

1½ cups grated *asadero* cheese, or jack cheese

¼ cup chopped jalapeño chiles, seeds and stems removed

¼ cup sliced stuffed green olives

Of course you can prepare this appetizer under the broiler, but since I use the grill to cook just about everything, why not use it? • **Yield: About 6 to 8 servings**

Prepare the grill for direct cooking at about 275°F.

Fry the tortillas in 1½ inches oil at 350°F, until crispy. Remove and drain on paper towels.

Arrange the tortillas on a pan or ovenproof plate. Top with the tomatoes, cheese, chiles, and olives.

Put the nachos on the grill, covered, until the cheese melts.

Full Court Press
Grilled Pork Loin Salad

**Year-Round Barbecue Rub
(page 277)**

Olive oil

**2 pounds boneless smoked
fully cooked pork loin**

**The Sun-Dried Tomato
Vinaigrette**

**12 sun-dried tomatoes,
chopped**

**2 tablespoons chopped
Italian parsley**

**1½ tablespoons chopped
cilantro**

4 green onions, chopped

**½ teaspoon coarsely
ground black pepper**

¼ teaspoon salt

½ cup white wine vinegar

⅛ cup balsamic vinegar

1¼ cups olive oil

The Salad

**Mixed greens such as
spinach and romaine
lettuce**

**2 cucumbers, peeled and
julienned**

**1 small onion, sliced and
separated into rings**

**Quartered tomatoes for
garnish**

If I have to eat a salad, it might as well have pork loin on it. • **Yield: 6 servings**

Note: This recipe requires advance preparation.

Mix the rub with the olive oil in the proportion of 1 tablespoon dry rub to 1 teaspoon oil. Rub the mixture over the pork loin, wrap with plastic, and marinate in the refrigerator overnight.

Combine all the ingredients for the vinaigrette in a jar and mix well. Allow to sit for 1 hour to mix the flavors.

Prepare the grill for direct cooking at high heat. Slice the loin into ¼-inch slices and grill for 30 seconds on each side.

Toss the vinaigrette with the greens, cucumber, and onion and place in salad bowls. Place the grilled pork slices over the greens. Garnish with quartered tomatoes.

No-Foul Chicken Fajitas
with Grilled Onion Guacamole

The Marinade

3 jalapeño chiles, minced

¼ teaspoon ground cayenne pepper

1 large onion, sliced

3 shallots, chopped

1 small bunch cilantro, chopped

2 teaspoons crushed black pepper

2 cups dark beer

⅔ cup corn oil

4 boneless, skinless chicken breasts

8 warm flour tortillas

Grilled Onion Guacamole (page 296)

People say there's no such thing as chicken fajitas because fajitas can only be made with skirt steak. Here's proof that they're wrong. • **Yield: 4 servings**

Combine the marinade ingredients and divide the mixture in half, reserving half for later use in the recipe.

Combine the chicken breasts and half of the marinade in a bowl and marinate for 2 hours in the refrigerator.

Prepare the grill for indirect cooking at 300°F, using apple wood for flavor, then direct and hot to finish. Remove the breasts from the marinade and cook for 30 minutes. Discard that marinade.

Remove the breasts from the grill and place in a bowl with the reserved marinade. Put in the refrigerator for 1 more hour.

Remove the chicken from the marinade and grill on one side for 4 minutes. Turn and grill the other side for 3 minutes.

When done, cut the breasts into thin strips. Serve the chicken with flour tortillas and the guacamole and allow your guests to roll the fajitas to their liking.

Slam-Dunk Dessert: Bread Pudding with Tequila Sauce

The Pudding

½ pound stale French bread

1 cup milk

1 stick butter, melted

½ cup golden raisins

¼ cup pine nuts

3 eggs, beaten

1¼ cups sugar

One 4-ounce can evaporated milk

One 8¼-ounce can crushed pineapple with juice

1 tablespoon freshly squeezed lemon juice

1 tablespoon vanilla

The Sauce

1 cup sugar

1 egg

1 stick butter, melted

⅓ cup good-quality tequila

1 teaspoon freshly squeezed lime juice

Does it seem that I use a lot of alcoholic beverages in my cooking? Maybe I should speak with my therapist about that. His office is at the Hooters in Tampa.

• Yield: 8 to 10 servings

Preheat the oven to 350°F. Break the bread into bite-size chunks and soak them in the milk for a few minutes. Squeeze the bread to eliminate excess liquid and discard the milk.

Place the bread in a large bowl and add the remaining pudding ingredients. Mix thoroughly but gently. Pour the mixture into an 8 × 12-inch buttered baking pan and bake for 1 hour, or until a knife inserted in the center comes out clean.

While the pudding is cooking, make the tequila sauce. Cream the sugar and egg together in a bowl. Add the butter and pour into a medium saucepan. Over low heat, stir the mixture until the sugar is dissolved. Remove from the heat and stir in the tequila and lime juice.

Pour the tequila sauce over the individual servings of the bread pudding.

April Fool's Day:
Faux Food Follies

▼▼▼

Mark Twain once observed, "The first of April is the day we remember what we are the other 364 days of the year." Historians have tracked the origin of the day to the change to the Gregorian calendar in 1582, when New Year's Day was moved from April 1 to January 1. Some people in France never got word of the change and others refused to move the celebration from April 1, so they were referred to as "April fools" by everyone else. They were ridiculed, sent off on foolish errands, or made the subjects of practical jokes.

Such fooling around eventually became a tradition of playing pranks on the first day of April, and it spread to England and Scotland in the eighteenth century, and eventually to the American colonies. "Kick me" signs were attached to the back of people's shirts, clocks were set back an hour, and the conclusion was the jokester saying, "April Fool!"

In 2005, my friend Dave DeWitt announced on his Web site (www.fiery-foods.com) that scientists had created a hybrid of a chile pepper and a tomato called a Chilmato, and that they had accomplished the feat through genetic manipulation. The article included a recipe for Chilmato Salsa and a very believable picture. Dave was flooded with e-mail, half of the people writing "April Fool!" and the other half asking, "Where can I get seeds?" I didn't ask for the seeds, but I must admit I was looking forward to trying them.

The recipes that follow are designed to fool people at your party on April 1. I suggest that you prepare these in advance so that the guests won't see the ingredients you use. Besides being a great April Fool's joke on committed carnivores, these recipes are really good alternatives to keep in your back pocket in case someone shows up at one of your barbecue feasts with a vegetarian. I know the chances are slim, but you never know. It's also just a plain old nice thing to do for people so that they don't feel left out.

Too Faux Burgers

The Pulled Pork Hoax

Scammin' Fajitas

Fake Sugar Cookies

▼▼▼▼

Too Faux Burgers

1 small onion, chopped fine

3 cloves garlic, minced

1 cup grated beets

2 tablespoons almond butter

2 tablespoons soy sauce

2 tablespoons balsamic vinegar

½ cup water

1 pound tofu, squeezed dry, coarsely chopped

½ cup vital wheat gluten (available in health food stores)

4 hamburger buns

That is probably the worst pun I've ever made but it kinda fits here. The guests are expecting beef and pork and you give them tofu and seitan (see next recipe). Seitan is some bizarre fake meat product, but it's not bad.

• **Yield: 4 servings**

Prepare the grill for direct cooking at high heat.

Combine all ingredients in a food processor except the tofu and wheat gluten and pulse a few times. And the tofu and process until well mixed. Transfer the mixture to a bowl, mix in the vital wheat gluten, and form into burgers.

Grill the burgers until they are done, about 7 minutes per side, depending on thickness. Place on the buns and serve.

The Pulled Pork Hoax

1 pound seitan, cut into
1-inch cubes

Year-Round BBQ Rub
(page 277)

½ cup Blender Barbecue
Sauce (page 286), or
substitute your favorite

Salt and freshly ground
black pepper to taste

4 hamburger buns

I understand that seitan is pronounced "Satan," and that may account for its unpopularity among meat eaters. It could also be the fact that it's *fake meat*! I don't quite get the concept of a vegetarian who eats fake meat. Call me crazy, but, if you want to be a vegetarian, eat vegetables.

• Yield: 4 servings

Prepare the grill for indirect cooking at 275°F, using hickory wood for flavor.

Season the seitan pieces with the rub and place in a grill basket. Cook on the grill for 2 hours. Remove to a cutting board and finely chop.

Transfer to a bowl and mix with the barbecue sauce. Spoon on the buns and serve.

Scammin' Fajitas

⅓ cup freshly squeezed lime juice

⅓ cup soy sauce

⅓ cup red wine

2 tablespoons vegetable oil

1 pound tofu, squeezed dry and cut into 3-inch by ½-inch strips, or substitute seitan

1 onion, sliced and separated into rings

3 large jalapeño chiles, seeds and stems removed, sliced into thin strips

6 flour tortillas

½ cup grated cheddar cheese

½ cup diced avocado

Sour cream, if desired

This recipe can be made with either tofu or seitan. Who really cares? • **Yield: 6 servings**

In a bowl, combine the lime juice, soy sauce, red wine, and vegetable oil and mix. Add the tofu or seitan and marinate for 2 hours at room temperature.

Prepare the grill for direct cooking at high heat. Place the tofu or seitan in a grill basket and grill, shaking the basket every few minutes. In another grill basket, add the onions and jalapeños and grill until they are soft, about 15 to 20 minutes. Both baskets should be ready at the same time. Remove both baskets from the grill.

To assemble, place the "meat" on a flour tortilla, add the onions and chiles, and then top with the cheese, avocado, and sour cream, if desired. Roll up the tortillas and serve.

Fake Sugar Cupcakes

½ cup cocoa

½ cup boiling water

1½ cups sifted cake flour

1 cup Splenda Sugar Blend for Baking

½ teaspoon baking soda

¼ teaspoon salt

¾ cup butter

2 large eggs, lightly beaten

¼ cup milk

1 teaspoon vanilla extract

Confectioner's sugar

Now they've got fake sugar that's so close to the real thing that you can bake with it. Top off your fool's feast with these sugarless treats. • **Yield: 18 cupcakes**

Preheat the oven to 350°F.

In a bowl, combine the cocoa and boiling water, whisking until blended. Set aside. In another bowl, combine the flour, Splenda, baking soda, and salt. Cut the butter into the flour mixture with a fork or a pastry blender until crumbly.

Combine the eggs, milk, cocoa mixture, and vanilla in a small mixing bowl; add one-third of the egg mixture to the flour mixture. Beat at low speed with an electric mixer until blended. Beat at medium speed for 30 seconds or until the batter is smooth, stopping to scrape down the sides of the bowl. Repeat procedure twice.

Spoon the batter into paper-lined muffin tins.

Bake for 22 minutes, or until a toothpick inserted in the center comes out clean. Remove from the pan; cool completely on a wire rack. Dust with confectioner's sugar.

Tax Day:
Hard Times Barbecue

▼▼

April 15 is not a day to celebrate. If you owe the feds, you must somehow scrape up the money to pay them. If you are getting a refund, the government has been using your money interest-free for a year. Even if you're dead, it might cost your heirs to get tax experts' advice on filling out your return, and then you know how much of your income is going to fund pork barrel projects, like federal funding of a tattoo-removal program in San Luis Obispo County, California (I'm not making that up). So this is a menu for those times when you are a little short on cash but still want to barbecue.

Spare Change Salad

Grilled Chicken Po'Boy Sandwiches

Fried Bacon Corn

Poor Man's Special: Peas and Rice

Chess Pie

▼▼▼▼

Spare Change Salad

The Dressing

½ cup orange juice

¾ cup freshly squeezed lime juice

1 cup olive oil

1 teaspoon honey

2 shallots, minced

4 cloves garlic, minced

⅛ teaspoon ground cumin

Salt and freshly ground black pepper to taste

The Salad

4 lettuce leaves from the outside of a head of iceberg lettuce

2 cups chopped spinach

3 carrots, peeled and sliced to resemble coins

2 English cucumbers, peeled and sliced to resemble coins

4 Roma tomatoes, sliced to resemble coins

I have to confess that Janet of Party Planners of Lakeland suggested this recipe. The only reason I took her suggestion is because it's very inexpensive to make.

• **Yield: 4 servings**

To make the dressing, combine ¼ cup of the orange juice and ½ cup of the lime juice in a blender and puree. Drizzle in 1 cup of oil while this mixture purees. Pour the mixture into a bowl and whisk in the honey, shallots, garlic, cumin, and the remaining orange juice and lime juice. Season with salt and pepper if desired.

To make the salad, use the iceberg lettuce leaves as a "purse," with each leaf holding ½ cup chopped spinach. Top the spinach with the carrot, cucumber, and tomato "coins" and drizzle the dressing over them.

Grilled Chicken Po'Boy Sandwiches

A Recipe from Barbecue All Star Byron Chism

Byron is a friend of mine and is the creator and driving force behind the very successful seasoning blend called Bad Byron's Butt Rub. ("A little butt rub makes everything better.") Byron is a graduate of the prestigious Culinary Institute of America, but like so many of us barbecue guys, he just wasn't happy in a typical cooking situation. So he created Butt Rub and took to the barbecue circuit. Cooking as buttrub.com, Byron and friends have been one of the best and most consistent teams in the country. I asked him to create a po'boy recipe for me, knowing full well that he'd come up with a great one—and he did.

In Byron's words, "The po'boy, a New Orleans classic, is basically a stuffed French bread sandwich. Its name is believed to have originated in the Depression era, when oysters were a dime a dozen. Even a 'po'boy' could enjoy a crusty oyster sandwich for about twenty cents. A po'boy is traditionally made with oysters, shrimp, or roast beef and is served 'dressed,' which entails shredded lettuce, tomato slices, and mayonnaise. Nowadays it can be almost anything, including this delicious grilled chicken version."

• **Yield: 2 to 4 servings**

Note: This recipe requires advance preparation.

6 boneless, skinless chicken thighs

1 cup Po'Boy Italian Dressing Marinade (page 292)

Two 12-inch loaves of French bread, split in half lengthwise

Mayonnaise as needed

Shredded lettuce and tomato slices as needed

Salt and freshly ground black pepper to taste

At least 6 hours before you plan to cook, place the chicken thighs in a zip bag and pound each one with a mallet or rolling pin to flatten. In another zip bag, marinate the chicken with the Po'Boy Italian Dressing Marinade for several hours to overnight in the refrigerator.

Prepare the grill for direct cooking at high heat.

Remove the chicken thighs from the marinade and grill on a hot grill for 5 to 7 minutes on each side. The chicken should read at least 175°F on a meat thermometer when done. Remove the chicken to a cutting board and cut into thin slices across the grain of the meat.

"Dress" the French bread bottoms with mayonnaise, lettuce, and tomato. Place the chicken slices on top of the "dressed" French bread. Season with salt and pepper to taste. Replace the French bread tops. Cut the sandwiches in half and serve.

Fried Bacon Corn

5 slices bacon

3 cups frozen corn kernels

1 cup water

½ tablespoon brown sugar

2 tablespoons butter, cut into little cubes

1 tablespoon Louisiana hot sauce

Salt to taste

Here's another cheap recipe for Tax Day. It's amazing how the simplest dishes taste so good. Must be the bacon. • **Yield: 4 servings**

In a large skillet, cook the bacon until crisp. Remove the bacon to drain on a paper towel. When the bacon is cooled, crumble it.

Add the corn to the skillet and toss to coat with the bacon grease. Add the water and brown sugar. Cover and cook about 15 minutes over medium heat. Remove the cover and continue cooking until the water is evaporated.

Remove from the heat. Add the butter, hot sauce, and three-quarters of the bacon. Toss until the butter is melted.

Transfer to a bowl and top with the remaining bacon.

Poor Man's Special: Peas and Rice

¼ cup olive oil

1 rib celery, chopped

1 small onion, chopped

2 cloves garlic, crushed

1 jalapeño chile, seeds and stem removed, chopped

1 cup pigeon peas, soaked overnight in twice their volume of water (black-eyed peas can be substituted)

1 teaspoon dried thyme

1 tablespoon salt

4 cups water

1 can tomato paste

2 cups uncooked white rice

There are variations on this recipe found all over the world. It's basic fare spiced up with a hot pepper.

• **Yield: About 6 servings**

Note: This recipe requires advance preparation.

Add the oil to a large saucepan over medium heat. Add the celery, onion, garlic, and chile and sauté until soft. Add the peas, thyme, and salt and cook for 3 to 4 minutes. Add the water and tomato paste and bring to a simmer. Cover and cook for about 30 minutes, or until the peas are tender.

Add the rice and more water if needed. Continue cooking for another 30 minutes, or until the rice is soft and fluffy.

Chess Pie

1 stick butter

1 tablespoon all-purpose flour

1 cup sugar

1 teaspoon cornmeal

1½ cups milk

4 egg yolks, lightly beaten

¼ teaspoon salt

1 teaspoon freshly grated orange zest

1 prepared 9-inch pie shell, unbaked

Whipped cream for garnish

This is my kind of dessert. I don't usually like heavy, big desserts. Chess Pie is a simple recipe that is composed of ingredients that you should always have in the house. If you want to substitute something or fancy it up, go right ahead. The possibilities are endless. There are many versions of where the name came from, but I like the one that says that first it was Just Pie. That eventually became Jess Pie and finally Chess Pie. That sounds like a nice story so I'm going with it. • **Yield: 8 servings**

Preheat the oven to 350°F. In a saucepan, melt the butter over low heat. Stir in the flour, sugar, and cornmeal. Remove from heat. In a bowl whisk together the milk, eggs, salt and orange zest. When the sugar mixture is cool, fold the two mixtures together, gently but thoroughly.

Pour into the unbaked pie shell. Bake for about 1 hour, or until a toothpick inserted in the middle comes out clean. Set aside to cool for at least 2 hours.

Serve topped with whipped cream.

Earth Day:
Salt of the Earth Barbecue

▼▼

Ever since 1970, Earth Day has been celebrated on April 22. The celebrations and work we do that day are designed to make us consider our environment and how to protect it. Apparently, the action and attention focused around Earth Day has worked; since it's been in existence, the following progress has been made:

- Emissions of the 6 principal air pollutants tracked nationally have been cut by 25 percent.

- Over the past 20 years, monitored levels of nitrogen dioxide (NO_2) have decreased 24 percent.

- Acid rain air pollutants have decreased from 16 million tons in 1990 to 11.2 million tons in 2000.

Now the question arises of what to put on the Earth Day menu. Supermarkets push organic food, which is fine, but it's not that simple. There are now some great products being grown by local farmers that are free of all the usual growth hormone and steroid-type suspects, but many are also grown using heirloom stock. There are breeds of livestock and strains of vegetables that don't fit the corporate needs, but are terrific in small batches. I recomend seeking this stuff out. Not only are they great products, but you'll typically be supporting a true artisan who is preserving an old tradition. Hence the name "heirloom."

Other organizations have their own agendas too, such as Vegetarian Earth Day and Soy Earth Day. Here at Dr. BBQ World Headquarters, I have my own agenda: Feed the Earth Barbecue Day. What could be nicer than the sweet smell of real wood smoke circling the globe?

Mother Earth Mudslide

Southern Hot Links

Barbecued Kid Shepherd-Style

Roasted Poblano and Potato Salad

Earth Day Mud Pie

▼▼▼▼

Mother Earth Mudslide

1 ounce coffee liqueur

1 ounce vodka

1 ounce Irish cream liqueur

1 ounce milk

L et's make a toast to Earth Day with this refreshing drink of the appropriate color. • **Yield: 1 serving**

Place all ingredients in a shaker and shake well. Pour into a glass filled with crushed ice.

Southern Hot Links

2 pounds ground pork
(shoulder cut preferred)

2 pounds ground beef
(chuck preferred)

2 teaspoons red chile
powder (piquin for hot,
New Mexican for mild)

2 teaspoons paprika

2 teaspoons dried sage

1 teaspoon ground cumin

2 teaspoons dried basil

1 teaspoon anise seed

2 teaspoons dried oregano

Sausage casings as needed

Dr. BBQ's Race Day
Barbecue Sauce (page
285)

Here is our recipe for a typically Southern sausage made with ground pork and beef. For this recipe you will need a meat grinder with a sausage funnel, a tube that fits over the end of the grinder for filling sausage casings. You can also use a mixer such as KitchenAid, which has a grinder and a sausage stuffer attachment. When stuffing, fill the casings until the sausage segments are about 6 inches long. Then twist the casing and tie the sausages off with string. When you're all done cut the links apart with scissors. If you must, you can buy the meat already ground and form patties, but the links are better. Serve the links on buns with raw onions and barbecue sauce. • **Yield: 10 servings**

In a bowl, combine all ingredients except the casings and the sauce and mix well. Using a meat grinder with a stuffing attachment, stuff the sausage casings and tie them off.

Prepare the cooker for indirect heating at 200°F, using oak wood for flavor. Place the sausages on the grill in the smoker, and smoke at 200 to 220°F. for about 3 hours, or until the internal temperature reaches 170°F.

Remove from the smoker and serve with the barbecue sauce.

Barbecued Kid Shepherd-Style

Known in the Southwest as *cabrito al pastor,* barbecued young goat is a spring tradition that can be duplicated in a grill with a spit or in a smoker. The biggest problem is going to be finding a young, tender 12- to 15-pound goat, and you may have to search out butchers, farmers, or ethnic markets. You can also substitute a large leg of lamb if you can't (or don't want to) find the young goat. • **Yield: About 20 servings**

Sprinkle the rub all over the goat and rub it in thoroughly.

If grilling the goat, build a hardwood fire in a large barbecue with a spit, or use natural charcoal and hickory chips. Arrange the goat on a spit about 1 foot above the coals. You can use a motor to turn the spit, or turn it manually every 10 or 15 minutes. Cook until the internal temperature reaches 170°F, for well done.

If smoking the goat, prepare the cooker for indirect cooking at 225°F, using pecan wood for flavor. Put the goat in the cooker. Smoke for about 1 hour per pound, or until the internal temperature reaches 170°F.

To serve, slice the *cabrito* thinly and top with barbecue sauce. Serve with the tortillas, guacamole, and salsa on the side, or make tacos topped with the salsa.

Roasted Poblano and Potato Salad

4 poblano chiles

2 pounds red-skinned potatoes

¼ cup cider vinegar

1 large red onion, chopped

½ cup finely chopped cilantro

8 hard-boiled eggs, quartered

1½ cups Hellmann's mayonnaise

Salt and freshly ground black pepper to taste

What could be more earthy than potatoes?
- **Yield: 8 to 10 servings**

Wash the poblanos and dry thoroughly. Prepare the grill for direct cooking at high heat. Put the poblanos on the grill and cook until the skin is blistered all over. When the skin is almost uniformly blackened, put the peppers in a brown paper bag, fold the top closed, and allow them to steam in the bag for about 10 minutes. After the peppers have finished steaming, take them out and carefully rub the blackened skin off. Open the peppers up by making a slit in the side and remove the core and seeds. Slice the flesh of the peppers into ½-inch strips and set aside.

Wash the potatoes but leave the skin on. Fill a pot with enough water to cover the potatoes and bring it to a boil. Cook the potatoes in the boiling water until tender enough to be pierced with the tip of a knife.

Rinse the potatoes and allow them to cool slightly. Slice them into quarters and toss with the vinegar.

When the potatoes have come to room temperature, add the onion, cilantro, eggs, and roasted poblanos, tossing gently. When combined fully, add the mayonnaise and toss again, adding salt and freshly ground pepper to taste. If you prefer a creamier potato salad, add a bit more mayonnaise to taste. Chill before serving.

Earth Day Mud Pie

The Crust

1 cup all-purpose flour

1 stick butter

1 cup chopped pecans

The Second Layer

8 ounces soft cream cheese

1 cup confectioner's sugar

1 cup Cool Whip

The Third Layer

2 large boxes chocolate pudding

Cool Whip for topping

Here is the perfect dessert for the day.
• **Yield: 9 servings**

To make the crust, mix all the ingredients in a food processor. Spread into a 9 × 9-inch pan and bake at 350°F for 15 minutes. Allow to cool.

To make the second layer, mix the ingredients in a food processor and spread over the crust.

To make the third layer, cook the pudding according to directions on the box and cool. Spread on the previous 2 layers. Top with more Cool Whip and refrigerate until ready to serve.

Easter:
A Family Barbecue Feast

▼▼▼

For Christians, Easter is a big feast day because it ends the long forty-day Lenten fast when such foods as butter, sweets, and meats are traditionally not eaten. Here are some Easter food facts:

- Easter is the second-most important candy-eating holiday after Halloween. Sixteen billion jelly beans are consumed on Easter, enough to go around the world three times.

- The custom of giving eggs at Eastertime has been traced back to the Egyptians, Persians, Gauls, Greeks, and Romans. The egg was a symbol of life.

- The lamb is a symbol for Christ and has a long tradition of being served at Easter feasts.

- In southern Italy, oval sweets in the shape of eggs are traditional.

- Easter baskets, long before they were filled with jelly beans, chocolates, and marshmallow Peeps, contained special breads and eggs prepared for the Easter celebration. The baskets were taken to the church on the Saturday morning before Easter and blessed by the priest.

- Ham is also a favorite Easter food because the pig has always been a symbol of good luck and prosperity among Europeans.

- In England, hot cross buns and simnel cakes, a kind of fruitcake, are Easter favorites.

I always serve lamb at Easter along with a full table of sides.

Dr. BBQ's Green Chile, Smoked Turkey, and Orzo Soup

Caesar Salad with Hard-Boiled Eggs

Smokin' Leg of Lamb

Potatoes au Gratin

Grilled Asparagus I

Simnel Cake

▼▼▼▼▼

Dr. BBQ's Green Chile, Smoked Turkey, and Orzo Soup

2 to 3 tablespoons olive oil

1 small white onion, halved and sliced thin

2 to 3 cloves garlic, minced

6 to 8 New Mexican green chiles, roasted, peeled, seeded, and chopped coarsely

1 to 2 jalapeño peppers, roasted, peeled, seeded, and chopped fine

2 vegetable bouillon cubes (Knorr is the brand I use)

2 teaspoons salt

1 teaspoon dried thyme

2 quarts water

2 cups chopped smoked turkey

1 cup orzo pasta

This is one of my all-time favorite soups. I love the combination of the smoked turkey and the green chiles. Like many soups and stews, this is much better the next day. • **Yield: 8 to 10 servings**

In a 6-quart Dutch oven add the oil, sauté the onion for a few minutes, then add the garlic and all the peppers.

Sauté until everything is soft and cooking. Add the bouillon cubes, salt, thyme, and water. Bring to a boil and simmer for 30 minutes, stirring occasionally. Add the turkey. Bring back to a boil and simmer for 15 minutes, stirring occasionally. Add the orzo and bring back to a boil. Simmer for 20 minutes, stirring occasionally.

Taste and adjust the salt as needed.

Caesar Salad with Hard-Boiled Eggs

Salt

1 clove garlic, peeled and halved

1 teaspoon dry mustard

1 tablespoon freshly squeezed lemon juice

1 tablespoon Hellmann's mayonnaise

Hot sauce to taste

3 tablespoons olive oil

3 bunches romaine, washed and dried

1 tablespoon freshly grated Parmesan cheese, or more to taste

1 can anchovies

2 hard-boiled eggs, sliced

½ cup croutons

It isn't traditional to serve Caesar salad with hard-boiled eggs. The salad is traditionally made with raw eggs incorporated into the dressing. Since hard-boiled eggs are such a part of Easter tradition, I've settled on a new twist and a spicier salad that complements the leg of lamb perfectly. • **Yield: 6 servings**

Sprinkle a little salt in the bottom of a wooden salad bowl and rub the garlic all over the bowl. Add the mustard, lemon juice, mayonnaise, and hot sauce and stir with a wooden spoon until all the salt has dissolved. Add the olive oil and stir to mix the liquids.

Tear the romaine into small pieces and add them to the salad bowl. Mix well.

Add the cheese, anchovies, egg slices, and croutons. Toss well and serve.

Smokin' Leg of Lamb

1 whole leg of lamb, 7 to 8 pounds, bone in

15 cloves garlic, cut into large slivers

¼ cup olive oil

Salt to taste

Freshly ground black pepper to taste

Dried oregano to taste

Lemon Mop (page 299)

I love leg of lamb and I almost always cook it bone-in. Some things just taste much better when cooked that way, and leg of lamb is one of them. I like it kind of simple, the way my Greek friends in Chicago cook it. The traditional flavors are garlic, lemon, olive oil, and oregano. What more do you need? • **Yield: 8 to 10 servings**

Prepare the grill for indirect cooking at 300°F, or the smoker at 300°F using grapevines for flavor. (Apple wood will substitute.) With a pointy knife, stab the leg of lamb all over and insert a sliver of garlic in each slit. Rub the lamb with olive oil. Season liberally with the salt, pepper, and oregano. Place the lamb in the cooker.

Once an hour, open the cooker and soak the meat liberally with the mop liquid. The lamb is done when it reaches an internal temp of 155°F. This should take about 5 hours. Remove to a platter and once again apply the mop liquid liberally. Discard any remaining mop liquid. Tent loosely with foil and let the lamb rest for 20 minutes. Slice and serve.

Potatoes au Gratin

6 cups russet potatoes, peeled and cut into 1-inch cubes

3 tablespoons butter

3 tablespoons all-purpose flour

1 cup heavy cream

1½ cups milk

3 cups shredded jack cheese

4 slices bacon, cooked and crumbled

1 teaspoon salt

1 teaspoon finely ground black pepper

Paprika as needed

I like to make my Potatoes au Gratin a little differently than most folks. Instead of adding the cheese to the milk and flour, I like to mix it in with the potatoes and then pour the sauce over the top. The cheese gets spread around plenty but it stays separated enough to add an interesting texture. These do fine in the oven but also do well in the barbecue cooker, for an added little smoky taste.

• **Yield: 6 to 8 servings**

Preheat the oven or cooker to 350°F.

Drop the potatoes into a kettle of boiling salted water. Return to a boil and cook for about 3 minutes, until fork tender. Drain and transfer to a large bowl.

Meanwhile, melt the butter in a medium saucepan. Blend in the flour. Add the cream and milk and cook, stirring occasionally, until it comes to a boil and thickens. Remove from the heat.

Add the cheese and the bacon to the potatoes and toss to mix. Transfer to a greased 9 × 13-inch pan. Spread all the ingredients evenly. Sprinkle with salt and pepper. Pour the sauce over the potatoes. Gently shuffle the potatoes to get the sauce evenly distributed. Sprinkle lightly with paprika. Cook for about 45 minutes until browned and bubbling.

Grilled Asparagus I

2 pounds fresh, thin
asparagus, woody ends
removed

¾ cup olive oil

Juice of 1 lemon

Salt and pepper to taste

If you're lucky and Easter doesn't come too early (by the way, did you ever notice that Easter is usually "early" or "late" but never "right on time"?), slim green spears of fresh asparagus will begin appearing in the stores. And there's nothing better with a roasted leg of lamb than a dish of lightly grilled asparagus. Here's the first version of this grilled favorite (another comes later), simple and easy.

• **Yield: 6 to 8 servings**

Prepare the grill for direct cooking at high heat.

Toss the asparagus with ¼ cup of the olive oil. When the grill is hot, place the asparagus spears directly on the grill or on the grill pan.

Carefully toss and turn them on the grill for about 8 to 10 minutes, until cooked through and slightly charred here and there. Remove to a platter, lining them up nicely.

Combine the remaining olive oil and the lemon juice and pour over the asparagus. Sprinkle with salt and freshly ground pepper to taste. Serve at room temperature.

Simnel Cake

1 cup margarine, softened

1 cup light brown sugar

4 eggs

1¾ cups self-rising flour

1⅓ cups golden raisins

1 cup dried currants

⅔ cup candied cherries, rinsed, dried, and quartered

¼ cup candied mixed fruit peel, chopped

2 tablespoons grated lemon zest

¼ teaspoon ground cinnamon

1 teaspoon ground nutmeg

½ teaspoon ground allspice

½ teaspoon ground ginger

1 pound almond paste

2 tablespoons apricot jam

1 egg, beaten

Here is the traditional Easter dessert from England. The 11 almond paste balls represent the 11 apostles, excluding Judas. • **Yield: 8 servings**

Preheat the oven to 300°F. Grease and flour an 8-inch springform pan. Line the bottom and sides of the pan with greased parchment paper.

In a large bowl, cream together the margarine and brown sugar until light and fluffy. Beat in the eggs, 1 at a time, and then the flour. Add the raisins, currants, candied cherries, mixed fruit, lemon zest, cinnamon, nutmeg, allspice, and ginger and stir well. Pour half of the batter into the prepared pan.

Divide the almond paste into 3 equal portions. Roll out one-third of the almond paste to an 8-inch circle. Place the circle of almond paste on the cake batter in the pan. Cover with the remaining cake batter.

Bake in the oven for 2½ hours, or until evenly brown. Remove from the oven and let cool in the pan for 10 minutes; then turn out onto a wire rack and cool completely. Set the oven to broil.

When the cake has cooled, brush the top with warmed apricot jam. Roll out the second one-third of the almond paste into an 8-inch circle and place it on top of the cake. Divide the remaining one-third of almond paste into 11 pieces and roll into balls. Brush the almond paste on top of the cake with beaten egg. Arrange the 11 balls around the outside edge on the top of cake. Brush the balls lightly with egg.

Place the cake under the broiler until the almond paste is golden brown, about 8 minutes.

May Day:
Another Excuse to Barbecue

▼▼▼

Fertility festival or labor festival? Well, May Day, the first of May, is both. It started off in ancient times as a spring festival to honor rebirth and fertility, and the maypole that was danced around was said to represent the tree of life as well as the male procreative organ. (Notice how delicately I put that.)

May Day as a celebration of labor started in 1886 when about 200,000 workers across the United States went on strike for an eight-hour workday. This led to demonstrations and strike-breaking in Chicago and caused the infamous Haymarket Affair in which police and workers were killed, and the supposed ringleaders were hanged. This situation inspired workers around the world, and May Day became symbolic to socialists and communists. It used to be the excuse for the old Soviet Union to stage scary military parades in Red Square, and today it is still celebrated around the world. You'll see parades with big missiles and such on this day. The phallic theme continues. Ironically, May Day's symbolism for workers has been upstaged by Labor Day, which pretends that workers and management are all happily working on the same team.

For my May Day barbecue menu, I've tried to lighten things up a bit.

May Day Punch

Grilled Salmon Steaks with Green Chile Lime Sauce

Corn and Potato Cakes with Poblano Vinaigrette

Luncheon Cake

▼▼▼▼▼

May Day Punch

½ cup passion fruit juice, made from the pulp of fresh passion fruits, or substitute ¼ cup concentrate

¼ cup freshly squeezed lime juice

3 cups white grape juice

2 cups pineapple juice

Two 12-ounce cans ginger ale

Lime slices for garnish

In honor of the original meaning of May Day, why not use passion fruit in a refreshing punch? Of course, it would be good to add a bit of rum to this punch.

• Yield: 4 to 6 servings

Combine all the ingredients except the lime slices in a pitcher and mix well. Serve in tall glasses filled with crushed ice and garnished with lime slices.

Grilled Salmon Steaks
with Green Chile Lime Sauce

4 salmon steaks

Olive oil

Salt and freshly ground
black pepper

The Sauce

½ cup chopped fresh
cilantro leaves

3 New Mexican green
chiles, stems and seeds
discarded, roasted and
peeled

2 cloves garlic, chopped

Juice of 1 lime

1 tablespoon vegetable oil

1 teaspoon freshly grated
lime zest

Here is a simple salmon recipe that's quick to prepare but tastes great. You can whip up the sauce while you are starting the grill. • **Yield: 4 servings**

Prepare the grill for direct coking at medium heat, using apple wood for flavor.

Brush the steaks with the oil and season with the salt and pepper.

Place all the ingredients for the sauce in a blender or food processor and puree until smooth.

Grill the steaks over a medium fire for about 8 minutes, turning several times, or until the fish flakes on the outside.

To serve, pour some of the sauce on individual plates, place the steaks on top of the sauce, and top with additional sauce.

Corn and Potato Cakes
with Poblano Vinaigrette

1 small red onion, diced

1 tablespoon butter

3 russet potatoes

1 ear sweet corn, grilled
until slightly blackened,
kernels removed from cob

¼ cup plain nonfat yogurt

2 teaspoons ancho chile
powder, or substitute New
Mexican chile powder

Kosher salt and freshly
ground pepper to taste

3 tablespoons butter

Poblano Vinaigrette (page
297)

I love this recipe because it sounds so elegant yet is really simple to prepare. • **Yield: 4 servings**

To make the potato cakes, add the onion and butter to a pan and sauté until the onion has browned slightly.

Steam or boil the potatoes for 25 to 30 minutes with skins on. Peel while still warm and mash coarsely in a mixing bowl. Add the onion, corn, yogurt, chile, salt, and pepper and mix well. Spread the mixture ¾-inch thick on a 9 × 9-inch baking pan. Cool in the refrigerator, and then, using a 2-inch circular cutter, cut out cakes.

Melt the butter in a pan and sauté the potato cakes until golden brown on each side.

Divide the vinaigrette equally among 4 plates; the vinaigrette should cover the bottom of each plate. To serve, stand three corn cakes on edge. Repeat procedure with remaining plates and ingredients.

Luncheon Cake

A Recipe from Barbecue All Star Stephanie Wilson

1 box yellow cake mix

2 packages instant vanilla pudding

Two 15-ounce cans crushed pineapple, drained

1 large tub Cool Whip

Yellow sprinkles

Stephanie, or Steph, is the office manager at the Kansas City Barbeque Society. The staff isn't very big, so that means Steph and her trusty sidekick Sybilla do everything from editing the monthly KCBS newspaper, *The Bullsheet,* to painting the bathroom. They do a great job of keeping things in order around the place. It's not an easy job considering the wild growth that KCBS and barbecue cookoffs in general are experiencing. Steph is also a good friend of mine and a world-class barbecue cook. Steph, her son Brent, her sister Valerie, and Kyle Laval cook as The Slabs, and they are one of the top teams anywhere. I asked her for a dessert recipe and she gave me this one. When I asked where it came from, she said her uncle Joe gave it to her. Thanks to both of them. • **Yield: 12 servings**

Prepare the cake mix in a 9 × 13-inch pan per the package directions. Cool.

Prepare the pudding per the package directions and set aside. Spread the crushed pineapple evenly over the cake. Spread the prepared pudding evenly over the pineapple. Spread the Cool Whip over the pudding. Top with the yellow sprinkles.

A Springtime Picnic:
Portable Grilling

▼▼

Many picnic sites have their own charcoal grills, which are handy for cooking outside. Just pick a day when the spring winds aren't blowing. There are some small grill units that you can pack up and take with you—hibachis and the handy little Cobb grills come to mind.

If you have kids, the notion of removing them from their iPods in order to commune with nature can be daunting. Just remember that before video games, kids had fun playing volleyball and badminton, so it might not be a bad idea to revive those two activities on your picnic.

Just about any outdoor location away from home is appropriate for your picnic. But here are a few places you might want to avoid:

- private property
- landfills
- cemeteries
- swamps
- dark alleys
- chemical dumps
- Death Valley in the summer

One other thing to watch out for are packs of roving wild dogs. They're usually not good picnic guests.

Stay away from these things and you'll have a great picnic.

Grilled Fruit Kabobs

Pulverized Goldfish Burgers

Ginger–Macadamia Nut Brownies

▼▼▼▼▼

Grilled Fruit Kabobs

1 fresh pineapple, cored and cut into bite-size chunks

2 pounds seedless grapes

6 peaches, pitted and cut into bite-size chunks

6 bananas, peeled and cut into bite-size chunks

1 cup brown sugar

1 cup orange juice

18 to 24 bamboo skewers, soaked in water for at least 1 hour

I love grilled fruit. It's easy to prepare because all you really need to do is warm it up. I like to make up these kabobs and carry them to a picnic in a plastic container all ready for a quick grilling. • **Yield: 18 to 24 skewers**

Thread the fruit on the skewers in alternating fashion. Place the prepared kabobs in a plastic container. Combine the orange juice with the brown sugar and pour over the skewered fruit. Refrigerate for at least 4 hours and up to overnight.

Prepare the grill for direct cooking at high heat. Place the fruit kabobs directly on the grate and cook for about 2 minutes. Turn and cook another 2 minutes. If your grill is hot, they will be browned and done. If not, just cook them another couple of minutes. Avoid overcooking because they will fall apart.

Pulverized Goldfish Burgers

1½ pounds ground chuck

¾ cup pulverized Goldfish (the little orange crackers, that is)

2 tablespoons salt

1 teaspoon onion powder

1 teaspoon finely ground black pepper

½ teaspoon garlic powder

4 eggs, lightly beaten

This idea came to me when I woke up in the middle of the night. You just never know where your inspiration will come from. I've been a fan of singer/songwriter John Prine for a long time and I've seen him many times in concert. I once heard him introduce a song by saying he'd written it on his tour bus in the parking lot of a closed-down mall in Virginia. "You gotta write 'em somewhere" was his explanation. I'm no John Prine, but some days I feel the same way.

The great thing about bringing these to a picnic is that the cheese and onion are already in there. Just bring along the ketchup and mustard, or better yet, some barbecue sauce.

• **Yield: 6 servings**

In a big bowl, combine all the ingredients and mix them well. You'll need to get your hands dirty on this one. Now make 6 patties all the same size, being sure to smash down the middle so they won't turn into meatball burgers. Place them on a baking sheet and put them in the freezer. When they're firm enough to handle, put them between layers of wax paper or aluminum foil. Put them in a plastic container and keep them in the refrigerator or on ice until you're ready to cook them.

Prepare the grill for direct cooking at high heat. Put the burgers directly on the grill. Cook for 5 to 7 minutes per side or until they reach an internal temp of 155°F. Remove to a platter and serve on toasted buns.

Ginger-Macadamia Nut Brownies

¾ cup unsalted butter, cut into pieces

4 ounces unsweetened chocolate, chopped

1 teaspoon instant coffee powder

3 large eggs

1½ cups brown sugar, packed

2 teaspoons vanilla extract

¼ teaspoon salt

1 cup all-purpose flour

1 cup chopped macadamia nuts

¼ cup crystallized ginger, minced

It's a little difficult to bake on a picnic, so I suggest that you make these ahead and just bring them along.

• **Yield: 16 brownies**

Preheat the oven to 325°F. Butter an 8 × 8 × 2-inch glass baking dish.

Mix the butter, chocolate, and coffee powder together in a heavy medium saucepan. Stir over low heat until smooth. Cool, stirring occasionally.

Whisk the eggs in a large bowl to blend. Mix in the sugar, vanilla, and salt. Fold in the chocolate mixture. Mix in flour, then the nuts and ginger. Pour the batter into the prepared dish.

Bake until a toothpick inserted into the center comes out with moist crumbs still attached, about 40 minutes. Cool in the dish on a rack. Cut into 16 squares.

Cinco de Mayo:
Southwestern 'Cue

▼▼▼

It all started because of a bad debt. In 1861, Mexican president Benito Juárez announced that all of Mexico's foreign debt payments would stop. This action made the French so mad that they invaded Mexico the next year. The plan was to capture Mexico and create a New World empire under the leadership of Napoleon III. The outnumbered, poorly trained, and badly equipped Mexican army whipped the six thousand–man French army in Puebla on May 5, 1862, which became known as Cinco de Mayo. It's a little-known fact that the French army regrouped and conquered Mexico, occupying that country for five years. But the French couldn't take the spiciness of Mexican food and eventually gave up and went home to their croissants.

Why is this Mexican historical moment celebrated more in the United States than it is in Mexico? There are a lot of theories that include Mexican immigrants to the U.S. and anti-French feelings here, but I have a hunch that it's the "any excuse for a party" syndrome rising up again. There's only a two in seven chance that May 5 will fall on a weekend, so Cinco parties often happen on Quatro or Seis, but, hey, it's another excuse for a barbecue.

The Perfect Margarita

Margarita Shrimp and Avocado Quesadillas

Barbecue Enchilada Casserole with Green Chile Barbecue Sauce

Grilled Zucchini with Chipotle

Tres Leches Cake (Three Milk Cake)

▼▼▼▼▼

The Perfect Margarita

1 Mexican (key) lime, or ½ Persian lime

Coarse salt

1½ ounces white tequila (I like Herradura)

¾ ounce Cointreau

Contrary to popular belief, the perfect margarita is not made with Triple Sec but with Cointreau. Also necessary for the perfect margarita are a great tequila and Mexican limes, also known as key limes. • **Yield: 1 serving**

Squeeze the lime into a shaker full of ice cubes. Rub the lime around the lip of an iced cocktail glass and dip the lip into coarse salt. Add the tequila and Cointreau to the shaker, shake well, and strain into the cocktail glass.

Margarita Shrimp and Avocado Quesadillas

The Marinade

¼ cup tequila

3 tablespoons Cointreau

2 tablespoons vegetable oil

1 tablespoon freshly squeezed lime juice

1 tablespoon chopped fresh cilantro

1 tablespoon finely chopped onion

2 serrano or jalapeño chiles, seeds and stems removed, finely chopped

1 teaspoon chipotle chile powder

1 pound small shrimp (26 to 30 per pound), peeled and deveined

Six 7-inch flour tortillas

Vegetable oil

1½ cups shredded Monterey Jack or *asadero* cheese

Chopped fresh cilantro

This is one of those dishes that can be served whole as an entrée or cut into wedges as an appetizer. Feel free to substitute chunks of chicken for the shrimp, if you like. Would you serve this with a margarita? Well, why not? I do.

• Yield: 12 to 18 wedges

Combine the marinade ingredients in a nonreactive bowl. Toss the shrimp with the marinade and refrigerate for 1 hour.

Prepare the grill for direct grilling at medium heat.

Place the shrimp in a grilling basket and place over the fire, shaking the basket often to make sure the shrimp are grilled on all sides. Grill for about 4 minutes over a medium fire, or until the shrimp just turn pink and are opaque. Remove from the fire.

Brush one side of 3 tortillas with the oil. Divide the shrimp among each, putting the shrimp on the unoiled side, sprinkle with the cheese and cilantro, and top with the remaining tortillas. Press firmly together and brush with oil.

Grill the quesadillas for 3 to 4 minutes or until the tortillas start to brown and the cheese melts, turning once—carefully. Cut the quesadillas into wedges and serve.

Barbecue Enchilada Casserole with Green Chile Barbecue Sauce

12 corn tortillas

Oil for frying

Green Chile Barbecue Sauce (page 286)

2 cups shredded smoked brisket or pulled pork

1 pound cheddar cheese, grated

2 medium onions, chopped

Shredded lettuce and chopped tomatoes for garnish

I love enchiladas almost as much as I love barbecue. Here's the best of both worlds combined into a great dish. • **Yield: 6 servings**

To make the enchiladas, heat the oil in a small skillet. Using tongs, dip the tortillas, 1 at a time, in the hot oil for just a few seconds until softened but not crisp, then drain on paper.

To assemble, put a small amount of sauce on the bottom of a casserole pan, place 4 tortillas on top, next more sauce, then the meat, one-fourth of the cheese, and some of the onions. Repeat the procedure for 2 more layers, ending with the cheese.

Bake in a 350°F. oven for 15 minutes, or until the cheese melts. Garnish with the lettuce and tomatoes and serve.

Grilled Zucchini with Chipotle

4 tablespoons olive oil

3 medium zucchini, cut lengthwise in half

1 medium onion, cut into ¼-inch slices

1 tablespoon wine vinegar

2 canned chipotles in adobo, chopped

Chopped fresh cilantro or Italian parsley

One of my favorite chiles, the chipotle, gives a wonderful smoky-hot flavor to the squash.

• **Yield: 6 servings**

Prepare the grill for direct grilling at medium heat.

Rub 1 tablespoon of the olive oil on the zucchini. Grill the zucchini halves over medium heat until done, about 10 minutes. Keep them warm.

Heat the rest of the oil in a skillet and sauté the onion until soft. Remove and keep warm. Stir in the vinegar and chopped chiles and simmer the sauce for a couple of minutes to blend the flavors.

Place the zucchini on a plate and top with the onions. Pour the sauce over the top and allow to marinate for 15 to 20 minutes. Top with the chopped cilantro and serve either warm or at room temperature.

Tres Leches Cake
(Three Milk Cake)

The Batter

6 eggs, separated

2 cups sugar

2 cups all-purpose flour

3 teaspoons baking powder

½ cup whole milk

1 tablespoon vanilla

The Three Milks

1 cup whole milk

1 can evaporated milk

1 can sweetened condensed milk

1 small container Cool Whip

Chopped pecans

Nobody knows where or when this recipe originated, but it is very popular both in Mexico and Texas. This is my simplified, insanely rich Florida version.

- **Yield: 8 servings**

Preheat the oven to 350°F.

In a bowl, beat the egg whites until fluffy. Add the sugar slowly and keep beating. Mix in the egg yolks and beat for 2 more minutes. Add flour and baking powder and mix well. Add milk and vanilla and mix for 5 minutes. Bake in a greased 9 × 13-inch baking pan for 30 to 40 minutes.

While the cake is baking, blend the 3 milks in a bowl. While the cake is hot, poke toothpicks into the top to make holes and then carefully pour the milks over the top of the cake. Refrigerate until cool. Spread whipped topping on top and sprinkle with chopped pecans.

Mother's Day:
Barbecue for Mom

▼▼▼

Many people believe that a greedy greeting card industry invented Mother's Day as a way to sell more cards, but the truth is that President Woodrow Wilson signed a joint resolution proclaiming Mother's Day on May 8, 1914. Since then, every second Sunday in May has been devoted to Mom, and the day is the most popular of the year for dining out and making long-distance telephone calls. It's also soon to be a very popular day for barbecue.

My mom isn't with us anymore, but I will tell you that at one of the last meals we had together, she ordered the ribs. She was a fan of barbecue before I was. I remember her making ribs for her friends at my grandma's house by the river in Wisconsin. And in Chicago, I remember her driving to a neighborhood that she probably shouldn't have gone to, because she knew the best rib joint was there. I suspect I picked up my tendency to have the barbecue sauce on the side from my mom, because that's how she always ordered hers. She also taught me how to make chicken soup with dumplings, the way she learned from my Polish grandma. I still make it that way. So this menu is for my mom, Louise Lampe. She would have loved it.

Grilled Asian-Flavored Shrimp and Scallop Kabobs

Grilled Veal Chops

Grilled Asparagus II

Mom's Lemon Meringue Pie

▼▼▼▼▼

Grilled Asian-Flavored Shrimp and Scallop Kabobs

½ cup olive oil

2 tablespoons hoisin sauce

1 tablespoon soy sauce

1 teaspoon Sriracha hot chile sauce (or more to taste)

6 jumbo shrimp, peeled and deveined

6 sea scallops, about the size of a quarter

2 long bamboo skewers, soaked in water for at least 1 hour

ere's an easy, spicy seafood dish that your mother will love too. • **Yield: 2 servings**

An hour before you plan to cook, prepare the marinade. In a small bowl, whisk together the oil, hoisin sauce, soy sauce, and Sriracha. Place the shrimp and scallops in a zip bag. Pour the marinade mixture over them. Seal the bag and toss to coat. Refrigerate for 1 hour.

Prepare the grill for direct cooking at medium-high heat.

Remove the shrimp and scallops from the marinade. Wrap each shrimp around a scallop. Push a skewer through the shrimp/scallop combo, going through the shrimp twice. Put 3 on each skewer.

Place the kabobs directly on the grate and grill 2 to 3 minutes per side, or until the shrimp and scallops are opaque and slightly firm to the touch.

Grilled Veal Chops

4 bone-in loin veal chops, about 1½ inches thick

2 tablespoons olive oil

Dr. BBQ's Steak Seasoning (page 282)

You don't hear much about grilling veal, but I really like it. You will probably have to go to a specialty butcher shop to find these chops. • **Yield: 4 servings**

Prepare the grill for direct cooking at high heat.

Brush the chops with the oil and season them liberally with the steak seasoning. Grill the chops for 3 minutes. Rotate (don't flip) the chops 90 degrees. This will help make those nice crosshatch grill marks. Cook another 3 minutes and now flip. Cook for about 6 minutes and test for doneness. I like mine about 130°F or medium rare. If you don't have a good thermometer, just cut a little slash near the bone and see if they are done to your liking.

Grilled Asparagus II

¼ cup balsamic vinegar

¾ cup olive oil

1 teaspoon garlic powder

1 teaspoon onion powder

1 teaspoon salt

1 teaspoon freshly ground black pepper

1 teaspoon dried thyme

2 pounds fresh asparagus, woody ends removed

When asparagus is in season I use them many different ways. For this recipe I like to grill them first, marinate them, and then grill them again. I think it allows the marinade to get sucked up in the asparagus real well. • **Yield: 6 to 8 servings**

Prepare the grill for direct cooking at high heat.

In a bowl, whisk together all the ingredients except the asparagus. Transfer the marinade to a baking dish.

Grill the asparagus for about 3 minutes per side and then transfer them to the marinade. Toss to coat. At this point you can set them aside to be warmed in the oven at a later time, or you can let them rest for 15 minutes or up to a couple of hours and then grill them again. In the oven, they would need about 15 minutes at 350°F. On the grill, cook for another couple of minutes per side.

Mom's Lemon Meringue Pie

3 lemons

3 eggs, separated

1 cup sweetened
condensed milk

1 prepared 9-inch pie crust

6 tablespoons castor
sugar, aka superfine sugar

My mom hated oranges and loved lemons. Kinda weird, but true. She would go hungry before she'd eat anything with oranges in it, but she loved lemon meringue pie. • **Yield: 8 servings**

Preheat the oven to 350°F.

Using a microplane, grate the outside of the lemons, taking care to only grate the outer colored skin of the lemons and not the white pith. Reserve the zest.

Juice the lemons and reserve the juice.

In a mixing bowl, beat together the egg yolks, lemon zest, and lemon juice until the mixture becomes thick and creamy. Beat in the condensed milk and pour the resulting mixture into the prepared pie crust.

Using a clean bowl, beat together the egg whites and castor sugar until the mixture forms stiff peaks, being careful not to beat so much that the meringue mixture becomes dry. Spoon the meringue mixture over the lemon pie filling. Do not smooth the top. Bake for 25 minutes. Remove and allow to cool.

Summer

A Beautiful Time
for Barbecue

Memorial Day:
A Traditional Day for Barbecue

Father's Day:
Kids Grilling for Dad

National Barbecue Day:
Dr. BBQ's Birthday

Summer Camping Trip:
Gourmet Grilling

Summer Solstice:
Stonehenge British Barbecue

Canada Day:
A Great Day to Barbecue, Eh?

Independence Day:
A Fiery Fourth

Bastille Day:
Barbecue Français

Dog Days of Summer:
Featuring Various "Hot Dogs"

Labor Day:
The Heartland Grill

▼▼▼▼▼

No matter how much you get involved in barbecue as a lifestyle, summer is still the king when it comes to grilling, slow smoking, and the parties we call barbecues. The days are longer, the sun is shining, the weather is beautiful, and we're all in a good mood. That sounds like a good reason to have a party to me. I'm certainly no domestic goddess, but I do have a few ideas for summer barbecue-theme parties. These should make for some hot summer nights.

- An all-barbecue pot luck

- A neighborhood progressive party, where you wander around the neighborhood as a group, eating a different course and having a special drink at each house

- A sauce-tasting party. You cook a bunch of ribs and chicken, then use it to sample many sauces, brought by all the guests. These can be homemade or store bought. There are endless options available on the Internet.

- Toga party

- Bikini party (This idea comes from my younger days. I lived with three other guys in sort of a frat house situation. We had a New Year's Eve Party and told all the girls they had to wear dresses or skirts. I still can't believe they did.)

- Cookoff team-practice party

- Exotic beer–sampling party

- Ride 'em cowboy party

- Margarita party

- A luau (You can combine some of the recipes in this section for a Hawaiian feeling or go to my first book, *Dr. BBQ's Big-Time Barbecue Cookbook*, to learn how you can roast your own hog in the ground.)

These ideas can all be combined with the special celebrations I'm suggesting in this book. You have a bikini party on the Fourth of July. See how that works? I've hosted parties with most of these themes, but I must admit that I made a couple of them up just for you. Let me know how the ride 'em cowboy party works out.

The granddaddy of this concept is the barbecue vacation. Now, there are some who think my life has become one big barbecue vacation. They might be right.

The barbecue vacation has become a popular thing to do, kind of a search for the Holy Grail, or maybe it's the perfect rib. Kansas City is a popular destination with its legendary old joints; same with Memphis. North Carolina is often thought of as the birthplace of American barbecue, and of course you can't leave Texas off the list. You really don't need to limit yourself to the hot spots, though; there are gems all over the country. I recently spent a couple of weeks in Albuquerque. I found three great barbecue joints, and I heard about at least one more. Who knew? On more than one occasion I've driven one hundred miles out of my way to try a barbecue joint that I heard about. I also have stumbled across little barbecue places that are not very famous but should be. I can find some good in just about any barbecue, so it's always worth the drive. Barbecue cookoffs or barbecue dinners at churches and VFWs and such can be wonderful events, too. If you see a sign for one, by all means stop by. Even if the food isn't great, I'll bet the experience will be.

Some other things to include when planning a barbecue vacation are visits to national and state parks, where you can prepare some barbecues of your own if you bring your cooker. I once was touring South Dakota with my big trailer cooker in tow when we decided to go to Bear World. It's one of those drive-through zoos. When I drove up to pay they recommended that I leave my cooker trailer in the parking lot. They figured the bears would be climbing all over it. I was on a barbecue vacation with my sister and my nephew. We were taking the long way to the cookoff in Frisco, Colorado. It was a great trip.

Of course cookoffs are always a terrific destination to include on your vacation. There is a great list on the Internet at www.kcbs.us. Pick one out and start planning a vacation around it.

There are endless reasons to barbecue in the summer. I've listed some good ones here, even invented a new one for you. Well, that new one has been celebrated at my house for years as my birthday; we just renamed it National Barbecue Day.

Memorial Day:
A Traditional Day for Barbecue

▼▼

Memorial Day, which falls on the last Monday in May, traditionally kicks off the summer barbecue. It was first known as Decoration Day and was inspired by the flowers being placed on the graves of Union and Confederate soldiers after the end of the Civil War. On May 5, 1868, General John Logan, who was commander in chief of the Grand Army of the Republic, officially declared that May 30 was to be known as Decoration Day. In 1882 the name of the day was changed to Memorial Day and in 1971 the day was moved to the last Monday in May and was declared a national holiday.

I've long been interested in the origins of backyard grilling in the States and have some interesting books in my collection of barbecue cookbooks. One is the *Sunset Barbecue Cook Book*, and I have the second edition, printed in May 1951 with a cover price of $1.50. It's all over the place with the definition of "barbecue," including "skillet and kettle cooking," "oven roasting," and even "firepit cooking," which requires a permanent cooking pit in the backyard! There are grilled burgers, franks, steaks, and the like and instructions for grilling chicken, venison, lamb, and turkey. The sauces are actually pretty good. I also have a copy of *Retro Barbecue*, with amazing '50s grilling and lifestyle illustrations apparently taken from magazines of the time. The author re-creates the spirit of the era with Reuben Burgers, Drunken Ham, and Maui Wowee Luau Ribs.

Those two books inspired me to come up with my own retro menu for a Memorial Day cookout. For me, a retro barbecue involves the memory of my dad sipping a martini and cooking some giant steaks. That still seems like a pretty good start to a barbecue. Some things are just timeless.

Beefeater Martini, Straight Up

Garden Salad with Homemade Roquefort Dressing

Grilled Porterhouse Steaks

Sherry 'Shrooms

Dr. BBQ's Better Baked Potatoes

Peach Blossom Pie

▼▼▼▼

Beefeater Martini, Straight Up

2 ounces Beefeater gin

½ ounce dry vermouth (optional)

3 anchovy-stuffed olives

This one's for my dad. Martinis will never go out of style. And regardless of whether you prefer gin or vodka as the liquor of choice, it's difficult to just drink one.

• Yield: 1 serving

Fill a cocktail shaker with ice. Pour the gin and vermouth over the ice. Shake well. Pour into a martini glass. Garnish with the olives on a skewer.

Garden Salad with Homemade Roquefort Dressing

½ **head iceberg lettuce, washed and pulled apart**

2 ripe tomatoes, chopped

1 cucumber, peeled and diced

1 small sweet onion, chopped

1 carrot, peeled and diced

1 clove garlic, minced

1 tablespoon Dijon mustard

Salt to taste

¼ **cup white wine vinegar**

¾ **cup olive oil**

¼ **cup crumbled Roquefort cheese**

Many people don't realize that some salad dressings don't come from a jar. In the spirit of authenticity, I am calling for iceberg lettuce here, but you can substitute romaine, or even spinach if you like. • **Yield: 4 servings**

In a bowl, combine the lettuce, tomatoes, cucumber, onion, and carrot and toss.

In another bowl, mix together the garlic, mustard, salt, and vinegar. Whisk in the olive oil in a steady stream until the dressing is thick. Stir in the cheese.

Serve at room temperature on the side of the salad.

Grilled Porterhouse Steaks

4 porterhouse steaks, USDA Choice grade, at least 1½ inches thick

4 tablespoons Dr. BBQ's Steak Seasoning (page 282)

Here's another classic. There's just nothing like a big porterhouse steak. • **Yield: 4 servings**

Prepare the grill for direct cooking at high heat.

Sprinkle the seasoning evenly on both sides of the steaks.

Place the steaks directly on the grill. Cook for 4 minutes. Rotate the steaks 90 degrees. (This helps make the nice crosshatch grill marks). Cook another 4 minutes. Flip the steaks and repeat the process. Check for doneness along the way. I like mine pretty rare so I take them off at 125°F, but you may want to go to 135°F. Remove to a platter and serve.

Sherry 'Shrooms

2 tablespoons butter

1 tablespoon chopped
Italian parsley

1 clove garlic, minced

1 small onion, chopped

1 tablespoon all-purpose
flour

1 cup beef broth

⅛ teaspoon ground
nutmeg

1 pound button
mushrooms, left whole

¼ cup dry sherry

4 bamboo skewers, soaked
in water for at least 1
hour

Here is the perfect topping for the porterhouses.
• **Yield: 2 to 4 servings**

Prepare the grill for direct cooking at high heat.

In a saucepan, heat 1 tablespoon of the butter, add the parsley, garlic, and onion, and cook over medium heat for 3 minutes. Stir in the flour and then the broth. Add the nutmeg.

Thread the mushrooms on skewers or place them in a grill basket. Put them on the grill and cook for 5 minutes, turning often. Add the mushrooms to the saucepan, add the sherry, and simmer for 10 minutes.

Dr. BBQ's Better Baked Potatoes

4 large russet potatoes, scrubbed and dried

1 stick butter, softened

2 tablespoons minced fresh chives

1 tablespoon minced fresh Italian parsley

½ cup cooked, crumbled bacon

Baked potatoes make a great accompaniment for big steaks. You can do these on the cooker, too; just allow a little extra time. Russets are the best baking potatoes, so use them in this dish. I like the big round ones.

• **Yield: 4 servings**

Preheat the oven to 450°F.

Bake the potatoes in the oven for about 1 hour, or until they are easily pierced by a fork.

While the potatoes are baking, combine in a bowl the butter, chives, and parsley and mix well. Remove the potatoes from the oven, cut them in half lengthwise, and score the flesh with a knife. Top with the chive butter and sprinkle the bacon over the top.

Peach Blossom Pie

3 to 4 peaches, depending on size

1 unbaked 9-inch pie shell, chilled

2 eggs, beaten

1 cup milk

¾ cup sugar

1 tablespoon all-purpose flour

Pinch of salt

3 drops almond extract

So named because the halved peaches resemble flowers, this dessert is a classic from the '50s. It can be served with ice cream or whipped cream.

- **Yield: 6 servings**

Preheat the oven to 400°F.

Peel the peaches, remove the pits, and cut the fruit in half. Arrange them cut side up in the pie shell. In a bowl, combine the eggs, milk, sugar, flour, salt, and almond extract. Pour this mixture over the peach halves. Bake for 10 minutes, reduce the heat to 325°F, and continue baking for about 35 minutes or until a sharp knife inserted into the custard comes out clean. Serve either warm or cold.

National Barbecue Day:
Dr. BBQ's Birthday

▼▼

Since no such holiday exists in the world, I am proclaiming my birthday, June 5, as National Barbecue Day. I have prepared a delicious menu of my favorite things for this special occasion, but more importantly, I have some guidelines for celebrating this fabulous new holiday.

Things *not* to do on National Barbecue Day:

- Pass out too early.
- Go dancing.
- Catch yourself on fire.
- Gossip.
- Shave.
- Concern yourself with the evil things that good food is rumored to do to you.

Things you *should* do on National Barbecue Day:

- Give gifts to your favorite barbecuers. A brisket would be nice.
- Serve only the finest beers, wines, and liquors as is appropriate for the occasion.
- Eat only grilled or smoked foods and approved sides (those in this book).
- Read inspirational passages from this book to your assembled guests.
- Entertain by showing tapes of *All-Star BBQ Showdown* on OLN (Outdoor Life Network).
- Eat two desserts.

Finally, here's what I eat on my birthday, June 5, forevermore known as National Barbecue Day.

The Happy Doctor

Shrimp de Jonghe

Smoked Turkey (The Perfect Breasts)

The Best Corn on the Cob

Marsha's Buttermilk Pie

▼▼▼▼

The Happy Doctor

3 ounces Jack Daniel's Old No. 7 Tennessee Whiskey

12 ounces Coca-Cola

1 large tall glass with lots of ice

This is a one-sip cure for what ails ya.

• **Yield: 1 serving**

Pour the whiskey over the ice. Add the Coke. Stir.

Shrimp de Jonghe

1 stick butter

3 bunches scallions, chopped, most of the green reserved for another use

4 cloves garlic, crushed

1 pound large shrimp, peeled and deveined

½ cup sherry (something you would drink)

Juice of 1 lemon

1 teaspoon finely ground black pepper

½ cup breadcrumbs, divided

Salt to taste

Lemon wedges and chopped Italian parsley for garnish

Since it's my birthday, I'm going to buck up for some shrimp as an appetizer. I love Shrimp de Jonghe. Although it seems to have many incarnations, the constants seem to be lots of garlic, sherry, and of course shrimp. When I was a kid, my dad always made the family go out for Sunday dinner. His favorite place was called Northwest Halls on North Avenue and Western in Chicago. There was a really nice old lady cooking there named Eula, and my dad would always send a drink back for her. Then he would order the Shrimp de Jonghe. Her version was a creamy casserole, with lots of garlic and sherry. Cheryl Zak taught me how to make this version when she was living in Savannah, Georgia. It's quick and avoids overcooking the shrimp, which is key to me. • **Yield: 4 to 6 servings**

In a large skillet over medium heat, melt the butter. Add the scallions and the garlic and sauté for about 5 minutes, or until the onions are soft.

Add the shrimp in a single layer. Cook about 3 minutes or until the bottoms of the shrimp are pink. Flip the shrimp and cook another 3 minutes.

Add the sherry, lemon juice, and black pepper, bring to a simmer, and cook another 2 minutes. Now add as many breadcrumbs as you need to soak up the juices, but not so many as to make it dry. Check for salt and add if needed.

Remove from the heat and spoon on individual plates to serve. This isn't the prettiest version, so I usually garnish it with lemon wedges and chopped parsley.

Smoked Turkey
(The Perfect Breasts)

2 bone-in turkey breasts, 5 to 7 pounds, defrosted

4 tablespoons olive oil

Dr. BBQ's Chicken Seasoning (page 281)

Barbecue sauce for serving

Turkey is what I order most of the time in a barbecue restaurant, and I really like breasts, so that's what I have on my birthday. I like it pretty simple. The trick is to cook it at a little higher than normal smoking temperature, and get it off as soon as it's done. It will only get dry if you overcook it. • **Yield: 12 to 16 servings**

Prepare the cooker for indirect cooking at 325°F, using cherry wood for flavor.

Rub the olive oil all over the breasts, inside and out. Sprinkle the seasoning liberally all over the breasts, inside and out. This will really arouse the flavor of the breasts.

Place the large aroused breasts directly on the grill with the round and voluptuous side up. Cook to an internal temp of 160°F, no higher. This should take about 2 hours, but the temp is critical for the perfect breasts. Remove to a platter, tent loosely with foil, and let rest for 15 minutes.

Unveil the beautiful breasts. Slice and serve with barbecue sauce on the side.

The Best Corn on the Cob

12 ears fresh corn on the cob, husks and silk removed

1 tablespoon salt

Real butter and salt to treat the corn

Everybody knows that the best corn on the cob is from Wisconsin, and it's only available during a couple of months during the summer. I'm not a big green-veggie guy, but fresh corn on the cob might be my absolute favorite food. I usually plan a vacation around it, like some people do for Stone Crab Season and Hatch Chile Season. My brother-in-law Dino and I have been known to down a dozen ears during dinner. Unfortunately, National Barbecue Day is a little early for the great Wisconsin corn, but they do grow some pretty good stuff in southern Illinois, so that will have to do. Come July, head to Wisconsin and try the good stuff. I like it best boiled or steamed. Grilled corn is fun, but not the best eating. I also know cooks who add milk or sugar to the water. If you have the good corn from Wisconsin, there is just no need for that. I've heard of folks who put mayo and cheese on their corn. What are they thinking? Don't do that.

• **Yield: 12 servings**

Put the corn in a large kettle. Sprinkle the salt over the top. Fill the kettle with enough cold water to cover the corn. Bring to a boil over high heat. Reduce to a simmer and cook for 5 minutes. Turn the burner off and cover the corn. Let it steep for another 10 minutes.

Drain the corn and serve with lots of real butter and salt.

Marsha's Buttermilk Pie

A Recipe from Barbecue All Star Marsha Russell

2½ cups sugar

5 tablespoons cornmeal

6 eggs, beaten

⅔ cup buttermilk

2 teaspoons vanilla

1 cup butter, melted

Two 9-inch pie shells, unbaked

Marsha Russell is my friend, and she cooks just the way I like to eat. Her Fried Green Tomato recipe is in my first book, and she will probably get to be in any other books I write, too. She lives in Lynchburg, Tennessee, and she works for Jack Daniel's.

I love simple desserts that aren't too thick, heavy, or chocolatey, so on my birthday, aka National Barbecue Day, we are having Marsha's Buttermilk Pie. • **Yield: 12 servings**

Preheat the oven to 350°F.

In a big bowl, mix together the sugar and cornmeal. Add the eggs, buttermilk, vanilla, and butter. Mix until blended well. Pour half of the mixture into each pie shell.

Place the pies on a baking sheet and put them in the oven. Bake for 45 to 50 minutes or until set.

Remove to a rack and cool completely before serving.

Father's Day:
Kids Grilling for Dad

▼▼

Although the first Father's Day was celebrated in 1910 in Spokane, Washington, it wasn't until 1966 that Lyndon Johnson signed a presidential proclamation declaring the third Sunday in June to be Father's Day. There has been the usual speculation that this was done to benefit the greeting cards industry. I don't think so. If we ever have a national Stepchildren Day, I'll get suspicious, but Father's Day seem legit to me.

I think most dads will enjoy the day best if they spend it with their kids. The recipes in this section are real easy so that the kids can help Mom grill for Dad. That's the rule: Dad can watch baseball and drink a couple of beers, but he must keep his hands off the grill. This is a perfect day to induct your kids into the Barbecue Brainwashing Program sponsored by Future Grillers of America.

The Easiest Grilled Quesadillas Ever

Chicken Handle Pieces with Peachipotle Barbecue Sauce

Cheesy Mashed Potatoes

Cherry Pie Beans

Hot Banana Sundae

▼▼▼▼▼

The Easiest Grilled
Quesadillas Ever

Twelve 10-inch flour tortillas

2 cups jack cheese

1 cup prepared salsa

These are really simple and great on the grill. I get everything ready to go and build them right on the grill. • **Yield: 6 to 8 servings as an appetizer**

Prepare the grill for direct cooking at medium-high heat. Lay 2 tortillas on the grill. Top each with ⅓ cup of cheese and another tortilla. In about 1 minute the cheese should begin to melt. Flip the quesadillas. Cook another minute or two or until all the cheese is melted. Repeat the procedure twice more. Remove to a cutting board and cut each into 6 to 8 wedges. Top each wedge with a spoonful of salsa.

Chicken Handle Pieces with Peachipotle Barbecue Sauce

12 chicken drumsticks

Year-Round Barbecue Rub (page 277)

Dr. BBQ's Peachipotle Barbecue Sauce (page 284)

Kids love drumsticks. My nephew Dan used to call them "handle pieces." I think that explains it. It's much easier for a kid to manage a drumstick than a thigh or a wing. So because our theme is for Dad to enjoy the kids today, we're having drumsticks for dinner.

• **Yield: 6 servings**

Prepare the cooker for indirect cooking at 300°F, using cherry wood for flavor. Season the drumsticks liberally with the barbecue rub and put them in the cooker. Cook for 1½ hours.

Brush with the barbecue sauce and cook another 30 minutes. Check for doneness. The drumsticks need to be cooked to an internal temp of at least 180°F.

Cheesy Mashed Potatoes

8 medium red potatoes, scrubbed, dried, and half the peels removed

½ cup milk, or more if needed

¼ cup cheddar cheese

¼ cup pepper jack cheese

Kids also love to smash potatoes, so this recipe should be a hit on Dad's Day. I like the flavor of red potatoes, so let's use some. • **Yield: 4 servings**

Place the potatoes in a large pan and cover with water. Boil the potatoes until tender, about 20 minutes.

Place them in a bowl, add the milk, and, using a potato masher, mash them until smooth. Add the cheeses and mix well.

Cherry Pie Beans

One 28-ounce can baked beans, half of the liquid poured off

1 cup canned cherry pie filling

1 tablespoon finely ground black pepper

The sweeter the better for barbecue beans, so let's add some pie filling. Thanks go to Myron Mixon from Jack's Old South Barbecue in Vienna, Georgia, where I first saw this idea when he was making Apple Pie Beans at a cookoff. • **Yield: 6 servings**

Prepare the cooker for indirect heating at 300°F, using cherry wood for flavor.

Combine the ingredients in an aluminum foil pan.

Place in the cooker for 1 hour.

Hot Banana Sundae

2 bananas

2 big scoops of vanilla ice cream

2 big scoops of chocolate ice cream

Chocolate topping

Whipped cream

2 maraschino cherries

I came up with the idea of grilling bananas on the Big Green Egg for a trade show. I'm always looking for something different to do at these events. I don't usually have ice cream so I just serve them with whipped cream. This banana sundae is the real stuff. • **Yield: 2 servings**

Prepare the grill for direct cooking at high heat.

Cut both ends off the bananas. Leave the skin on, but slit the skin top to bottom on one side only. Put the bananas directly on the grill and cook until the bottom is completely black. This should take about 5 minutes. Flip the bananas and cook until the other side is completely black.

Put 1 scoop of each ice cream in each of 2 bowls, or banana split dishes if you have them. Carefully roll the bananas out of their skins. Cut in half and place on the sides of the ice cream.

Top each bowl with chocolate sauce, whipped cream, and a cherry.

Summer Camping Trip:
Gourmet Grilling

▼▼▼

Let's go camping! We'll borrow the neighbor's Hemi truck and their thirty-foot, fifth-wheel travel trailer. It has triple bunk beds, a queen bed, a three-burner range with oven, a double-door refrigerator, a microwave oven, an indoor tub and an outside shower, and an AM-FM stereo with a CD player. We can bring our own TV, DVD player, and game player. Then we can drive to the Nature's World Campground and Casino, where we can park on level ground with *no mud* because the campground is paved. Now *that's* camping at its finest.

Well, not really. I'm not sure what you call it—maybe RVing or something, but certainly not camping. Camping is when you backpack into a national forest and grill freshly caught fish over natural hardwoods that you actually gather from the forest floor. There are no showers; you bathe with the fishes. You don't play video games, watch TV, or listen to the radio. You bring one of those books where you identify all the birds you've seen in your life. That should help you get a good nap in.

Needless to say, I don't think that would be much fun either. There are happy mediums, though. Find a campground that has a nice tent-camping area. That should have you away from the mega motor homes, but you'll still be able to take a shower. They will have a fire pit, so you can try your hand at cooking over a real wood fire if you want. They may have a grate you can use; if not, they are readily available in the camping supply section of many stores.

Here are some things to know about cooking with wood.

- You will use up more wood than you think, so collect a big pile of it.

- Use hardwood branches of oak or hickory. Avoid using pine or fir, which can impart a turpentine flavor to the meat.

- Have a jug of water standing by at all times in case the fire gets out of hand.

- Using a paraffin fire starter and smaller branches at first, make a fire of some size and let it burn down to hot coals. These will lose heat faster than you think because they are not as dense as charcoal coals.

- Put the grate in place and begin grilling. Add small branches as necessary to keep the coals hot.

- You can keep the fire going for warmth and dessert (see recipe, page 164).

- Before you leave the campground, pour water over the fire bed and make sure all coals are doused to the point that you can run your hands through the fire bed. Try to leave the land as you found it.

- Don't attempt this in a casino parking lot.

Pasta Salad with Smoked Ham

Grilled Greek Chicken

Pommes de Terre en Papillote (Spuds in Foil)

Outdoor S'mores

▼▼▼▼

Pasta Salad with Smoked Ham

8 ounces spiral pasta, cooked

1 cup cooked green beans

1 cup sliced cherry tomatoes

1 cup diced smoked ham

½ cup chopped red bell pepper

½ cup chopped sweet onion

½ cup sliced mushrooms

½ cup chopped celery

¼ cup chopped Italian parsley

Bottled Italian salad dressing, as needed

It's best to make this in advance and refrigerate it for your camping trip. • **Yield: 6 to 8 servings**

Combine all the ingredients in a bowl and mix well.

Grilled Greek Chicken

6 boneless chicken breast
halves

½ cup olive oil

½ cup freshly squeezed
lemon juice

1 tablespooon salt

1 tablespoon finely ground
black pepper

1 tablespoon dried
oregano

4 cloves garlic, crushed

Greek chicken is a very popular dish in the little mom-and-pop restaurants around Chicago. It was one of my early triumphs as a cook. It's loaded with flavor, and just a little exotic. It's typically done with chicken halves or quarters, but for the camping trip it will be easier to use boneless breasts. I like to put the chicken in one plastic container and the marinade in another. Then when the time is right, pour the marinade over the chicken. Then simply put the container back in the cooler and the chicken will be ready when you are. • **Yield: 6 servings**

Place the chicken in a plastic container or a zip bag. Whisk together the marinade ingredients and pour over the chicken. Toss to coat evenly. Let marinate at least 4 hours, or up to 24.

Prepare the grill for direct cooking at medium-high heat. Grill the chicken breasts for 5 to 7 minutes per side, or until they reach an internal temp of 160°F. You may baste with the marinade once when you flip the chicken, but then it must be discarded for food safety.

Transfer to a platter, drizzle with additional olive oil, and serve.

Pommes de Terre en Papillote (Spuds in Foil)

⅓ cup olive oil

1 medium onion, chopped

1 large green pepper, chopped

3 cloves garlic, crushed

½ teaspoon salt

1 tablespoon coarsely ground black pepper

2 cans sliced potatoes

These are a camping favorite in France. I like to use those canned sliced potatoes because they're already cooked, so there will be no al dente potatoes for our camping dinner. You can, though, substitute parboiled potato slices, if you'd prefer. • **Yield: 6 servings**

At home before your camping trip, prepare the vegetables to be added to the potatoes at the campsite. Heat the oil in a medium skillet. Add the onion and green pepper and sauté until soft. Add the garlic, salt, and pepper and remove from the heat. Let cool and transfer to a plastic container to store. Refrigerate.

When you're ready to begin cooking, prepare the grill for direct cooking at medium heat. If you're using canned potatoes, drain off the liquid. Put the potatoes in a big bowl. Add the previously cooked vegetables and toss well. Add a little more oil if needed.

Lay out a big double-thick sheet of aluminum foil. Put the potato mixture on the foil and fold it up into a packet. Seal the packet as well as you can. Put the packet on the grill, turning occasionally, until the potatoes are hot. The time will depend largely on the fire and grill setup you are using, but 20 to 30 minutes would be an estimate.

To serve, place the packet on a plate and cut the top open.

Outdoor S'mores

1 bag of marshmallows

Hershey's chocolate bars, as needed

1 box graham crackers

A globetrotting gourmet I know from the Southwest tells me that this dessert is named after the S'more (SUH-moray) tribe of southern Guyana, which raised the mallow plants in tropical swamps and cacao (chocolate) in the higher regions. Instead of graham crackers, the S'mores used stone-ground cassava crackers sweetened with honey. I'm not sure I believe this explanation. All I know is that these are a delicious and fun way to end the night in camp. For your authentic culinary adventure, use the campfire for a real kids' treat. • **Yield: However many you want**

Toast the marshmallows on traditional marsh willow sticks over a hardwood campfire and place them on a graham cracker with a piece of chocolate. Take a second graham cracker and carefully mash it on top to complete the s'more.

Summer Solstice:
Stonehenge British Barbecue

▼▼▼

The Druids celebrated the longest day of the year (usually June 21) at Stonehenge with ceremonies for *Alban Heruin,* "Light of the Shore." This time, exactly between the planting and harvesting of the crops, was the traditional season for weddings. This is because many ancient peoples thought that the "grand union" of the goddess and god occurred in early May. Since it was unlucky to compete with the gods, many couples delayed their weddings until June, and that month is still the favorite month for marriage today. In some traditions, newlyweds dined on foods and beverages that featured honey for the first month of their married life to encourage love and fertility. This tradition lives on in the name given to the holiday immediately after the ceremony: the honeymoon. There were many solstice festivities around the world, including nude river bathing in Sweden, bonfires in Germany, and kachina dances among the Hopi tribe of the American Southwest. Sounds like fun to me.

In our ongoing project of "any excuse for a barbecue," I recommend the nude river bathing, and the cooking of this menu from the 2004 World Barbecue Champions on the day of the summer solstice. You see, the 2004 World Champions are from England, the home of Stonehenge. No, I'm not kidding and I'm pleased to have played a small part in their success. Early in 2002, I was scheduled to do a barbecue cooking class in Lynchburg, Tennessee. The class was advertised in the Kansas City Barbeque Society's newspaper, *The Bullsheet,* which is sent to members all over the world. So one day I got a call from Rick Weight in England, asking if he and his wife could attend. I said, "Sure, we'd love to have you." Rick and his lovely wife, Jackie, came from England to Tennessee to take my cooking class! I've done many of these classes, and I don't think anyone has kept their focus the whole time as well as Jackie did. The class is long, and most folks skip out on a few sessions, but Jackie didn't miss a trick. So a year later they attended the Jack Daniel's World Championship Invitational Barbecue as an international team. They did pretty well, but all the big guns are there so they were out of their league. Well, apparently they went home and practiced pretty hard, because in 2004 they came back and won the whole thing. No international team had ever even come close to winning before. It was an amazing feat. They are great people and great cooks, and I thank them for this wonderful menu with an English influence.

Smoked Portobello Mushrooms with Goat Cheese and a
Red Onion Confit

Stuffed Tenderloin of Pork

Garlic, Lemon, and Thyme Roasted Chicken Breasts

Crushed New Potatoes

A Medley of Roasted Summer Vegetables

Summer Fruit Pudding

▼▼▼▼

Smoked Portobello Mushrooms with Goat Cheese and a Red Onion Confit

4 large portobello
mushrooms

2 red onions

Olive oil

¼ cup balsamic vinegar

¼ cup red wine

1 tablespoon honey

1 teaspoon vanilla extract
(not essence)

4 slices soft goat cheese
(½ inch thick)

Sea salt and freshly
ground black pepper to
taste

The dark and strong portobellos are the closest thing to meat in the plant kingdom. They go perfectly with goat cheese. • **Yield: 4 servings**

Prepare the grill for indirect cooking at 350°F. Remove the stems from the mushrooms, brush with oil, and put on the grill for about 15 minutes. Remove to a platter.

Peel and finely slice the onion into rings and fry them in olive oil in a skillet on the stove until softened. Add the balsamic vinegar, red wine, honey, and vanilla extract; bring to the boil to reduce the liquid until you have a thick, syruplike consistency.

Place a slice of goat cheese on each mushroom and top with the onion mixture. Season with a little sea salt and freshly ground black pepper. Return to the grill for another 15 minutes, or until the goat cheese starts to melt.

Stuffed Tenderloin of Pork

1 small red onion, finely chopped

5 ounces mushrooms, finely chopped

1 tablespoon olive oil

Pinch of dried sage

Pinch of dried thyme

½ cup fresh breadcrumbs

Grated rind of 1 lemon

2 tablespoons freshly squeezed lemon juice

¼ cup toasted pine nuts

4 tablespoons freshly chopped parsley

6 cardamom pods, seeds only, finely ground

3 teaspoons Asian sweet chili sauce (more if you like it spicy)

4 tablespoons chopped fresh cilantro

¼ cup very finely chopped dried apricots

Salt and freshly ground black pepper to taste

1 pork tenderloin, about 1½ to 2 pounds

Melted butter for brushing the meat

Fresh spinach leaves, tough stalks removed

Bacon

There's a little bit of work to making this dish, but the flavor is well worth the effort. Note that even though you are adding some wood for flavoring, the grill temperature is much hotter than with usual smoking.

- **Yield: About 6 servings**

Fry the onion and mushrooms in the olive oil until soft and transfer to a bowl. Add the sage, thyme, breadcrumbs, lemon rind, lemon juice, pine nut kernels, parsley, cardamom, chili sauce, cilantro, and apricots. Mix well and season with salt and pepper to taste.

Take the pork tenderloin and butterfly it (split lengthwise). Place a piece of plastic wrap underneath it and one on top and beat it out with a mallet to a thin square.

Remove the top piece of plastic wrap, brush the meat with butter, and lay spinach leaves so that the whole meat surface is covered. Spread the filling mix over the spinach—use your fingers to get an even covering.

Using the remaining piece of plastic wrap to help you, roll the whole thing up (similar to a Swiss roll or roulade). Dispose of the plastic wrap.

Wrap the bacon around the whole rolled piece of meat in a spiral so that you have completely covered the meat. Roll up with a fresh piece of plastic wrap and refrigerate until ready to cook (best to leave this for at least 1 hour to allow the flavors to infuse).

Prepare the grill for indirect cooking at 350°F, using cherry wood for flavor.

Place the meat on the grill and cook for approximately 1 hour, or until a meat thermometer inserted into the center reads 160°F.

Allow the meat to rest for at least 15 minutes and serve cut into approximately ¾-inch slices. *continued*

Note: The original version of this recipe includes blood sausage. I'm well aware that many people are squeamish about eating or using blood sausage, but it is standard fare in England and it can be truly delicious served alongside a pile of buttery mashed potatoes and a pint of good English ale. If you want to give this dish the authentic English touch Rick and Jackie do, add a blood sausage to the ingredient list. Then, before the roast is rolled up, take the skin off the sausage and lay it along the middle of the stuffing and roll it up. If you try it, I think you'll be surprised at the delicious flavor the sausage gives the dish.

Garlic, Lemon, and Thyme Roasted Chicken Breasts

8 sprigs fresh thyme

4 cloves garlic, finely chopped

Grated zest of 1 lemon

4 chicken breasts, skin on

6 tablespoons olive oil

2 cloves garlic, crushed

I'm always amazed when the simplest recipes taste so great. • **Yield: 4 servings**

Note: This recipe requires advance preparation.

Remove the thyme leaves from the stalk and combine them with the garlic and zest in a bowl. Mix well.

Loosen the skin from each of the chicken breasts and spread the garlic mixture under the skin.

Place the chicken in a shallow (nonmetallic) dish, pour the olive oil over it, and scatter any of the remaining garlic mixture over the skin. Crush the remaining 2 garlic cloves with the back of a knife and add to the oil and chicken to infuse.

Cover the dish with plastic wrap and refrigerate overnight or for a minimum of 6 hours.

Prepare the grill for direct cooking at medium-high heat.

Remove the chicken breasts from the marinade and place on the grill. Cook the chicken breasts, skin side down, for about 4 minutes, or until golden brown. Flip and cook about another 4 minutes, or until the internal temp reaches 160°F. Remove to a platter and serve.

Crushed New Potatoes

1 pound new potatoes

2 cloves garlic, finely chopped

Extra virgin olive oil as needed

Sea salt and freshly ground black pepper to taste

There's something about the aroma of garlic cooking in olive oil that drives me to salivation. Here is another simple but delicious recipe. • **Yield: 4 servings**

Boil the potatoes in their skins in a pan of water until cooked but still firm. Drain. Fry the garlic in a tablespoon of extra virgin olive oil until crisp but not browned.

Preheat the oven to 400°F.

Using a fork, break each potato so that they are very roughly crushed. Mix in the oil and fried garlic and transfer to a shallow dish. Top with sea salt and black pepper, then drizzle with a little extra virgin olive oil.

Bake at 400°F for 30 minutes, or until the top is browned and has a slight crust.

A Medley of Roasted Summer Vegetables

3 zucchini

1 large eggplant, peeled

1 green bell pepper, seeds and stem removed

1 red bell pepper, seeds and stem removed

1 yellow bell pepper, seeds and stems removed

2 sweet onions, cut into wedges

4 stalks celery

4 ripe plum tomatoes, quartered lengthwise

¼ cup extra virgin olive oil

¼ cup balsamic vinegar

1 tablespoon honey

Sea salt and freshly ground black pepper to taste

Fresh basil to serve

Here's one of my favorite veggie recipes and one where you use the grill like an oven. If your grill has a griddle, you could use it to cook the vegetables.

• **Yield: 6 servings**

Prepare the grill for indirect cooking at 350°F.

Prepare the vegetables and chop into chunks—they should all be about the same size so that they cook evenly.

Place all of the vegetables into a bowl. In a separate bowl, combine the extra virgin olive oil, balsamic vinegar, and honey; pour over the vegetables and mix everything together with your hands to ensure that all the vegetables are evenly coated. Season to taste with sea salt and freshly ground black pepper. Transfer the vegetables to a metal pan and place on the grill.

Cook for about 1 hour, or until the vegetables are al dente. You may want to toss the vegetables halfway through the cooking time.

Transfer to a platter. Tear the basil leaves and scatter over the vegetables just before serving.

Summer Fruit Pudding

1¼ cups raspberries

1¼ cups blueberries

1¼ cups strawberries

1 cup currants

1 cup castor sugar, aka superfine sugar

8 medium slices good quality white bread, crusts removed

Thick cream, crème fraîche, or a good vanilla ice cream for serving

The pudding can be made with any soft fruit of your choice (you will need approximately 2 pounds).

- **Yield: 8 servings**

Note: This dish requires advance preparation.

Prepare all the fruit (remove stems) and rinse.

Place the fruits with the sugar in a large saucepan and gently cook over medium heat until the sugar has melted and the fruit juices begin to run. This should take only a few minutes—don't overcook as you will lose the fresh flavor.

Lightly butter a 1½-pint pudding basin and line it with the bread—overlapping the edges and pressing down to ensure that you have a good seal. Fill in any gaps with smaller pieces of bread so that none of the juices can get through when the fruit is added.

Spoon in the fruit mixture, reserving ½ cup. Top with another slice of bread, again filling in any gaps. Place a plate on top of the pudding so that it fits just inside the rim of the basin. Place a 3- to 4-pound weight on top and refrigerate overnight. (Put the pudding basin in a dish in case of leakage.)

Just before serving, turn the pudding out onto a large serving dish and spoon the reserved fruit and juice over it, making sure you cover any bits of bread that still look white.

Cut into wedges and serve with thick cream, crème fraîche, or a good vanilla ice cream.

Canada Day:
A Great Day to Barbecue, Eh?

▼▼

On June 20, 1868, a proclamation signed by the Canadian governor general, Lord Monck, called upon all Her Majesty's loving subjects throughout Canada to celebrate the first anniversary of the formation of the union of the British North America provinces in a federation under the name of Canada on July 1. The July 1 holiday was established by law in 1879 under the name Dominion Day, which was changed to Canada Day on October 27, 1982.

Canada Day is a day of patriotic celebrations; most cities have organized parades, barbecues, and fireworks. The entertainment usually has a Canadian theme, Canadian flags are flown everywhere, and some wild and crazy people paint their faces in Canadian colors.

I do make a yearly trip to Canada, but not for the revelry of Canada Day. I go for the Canadian Barbecue Association Championship held every July in Barrie, Ontario. I'm honored to be the head judge at this event, with the help of Hope, the cutest redheaded Canadian girl I've ever met. She's smart, too. Well, smart enough to stay away from me anyway.

Smoky Deviled Eggs

Grilled Asian Vegetables

Peachy Pork Steaks

King of the Q Grilled Pineapple Upside-Down Cake

▼▼▼▼

Smoky Deviled Eggs

12 large eggs, hard boiled

Two teaspoons Year-Round Barbecue Rub (page 277), divided

½ cup mayonnaise

1 tablespoon hot sauce

2 slices bacon, cooked and crumbled

Salt to taste

Paprika for garnish

This recipe was inspired by Reg Pelletier. Reg is a Canadian barbecue cook whose team, The BBQ Boyz, won the inaugural Canadian Barbecue Association Championship in 2004. Then he went to the Jack Daniel's Invitational and won the "Best Cooking from the Homeland" award. Reg was the first guy I ever heard of making smoked deviled eggs. He cold-smokes a couple of the whole hard-boiled eggs for a long time, then mixes them in with the unsmoked ones. It's just not a practical technique for most home cooks, so I made a simpler version with his approval.

• **Yield: 24 servings**

Put the eggs in a pan with enough cold water to cover them. Bring to a full boil over high heat. Reduce heat to a medium boil and cook for 12 minutes. Remove from the heat and run cold water in the pan long enough to cool the eggs off.

Promptly chill the eggs so that the yolks stay bright yellow.

Prepare the cooker for indirect cooking at 200°F, using apple wood for heavy smoke flavor. Remove the shells from the eggs and halve them. Separate the yolks from the whites. Place 6 of the yolks on a piece of aluminum foil and sprinkle them with half of the rub. Place them in the smoker for 15 minutes. Remove and cool.

Put all the yolks in a bowl and smash them with a fork. Add the mayo, the remaining rub, the hot sauce, and the bacon. Mix until blended well. Add a little milk if the mixture needs some thinning. Check and add salt if needed.

Spoon the yolk mixture into the reserved egg white halves. Sprinkle with paprika and serve.

Grilled Asian Vegetables

1 cup snow peas

2 cups Chinese cabbage, chopped into ¼-inch pieces

1 can straw mushrooms, drained

2 scallions, cut into 1-inch lengths

2 teaspoons sesame oil

2 teaspoons freshly grated ginger

2 teaspoons minced serrano or jalapeño chiles

½ teaspoon salt

1 teaspoon sesame seeds

Vancouver has one of the largest Asian populations of any North American city. Here's a tribute to them with the essence of stir-fried vegetables and without the hassle of an extra pan to wash. • **Yield: 4 servings**

Prepare the grill for direct cooking at high heat.

In a bowl, combine the snow peas, cabbage, mushrooms, and scallions. Set aside. In another bowl, whisk together the oil, ginger, chiles, and salt. Coat the vegetables with the oil mixture. Place the vegetables onto four 12-inch-square pieces of foil. Sprinkle sesame seeds onto the vegetables, then fold into packets, doubling the edges to seal.

Grill on the edge of the grate, turning frequently to ensure that the vegetables are cooked evenly. Grill for about 10 minutes, or until the peas are al dente.

Peachy Pork Steaks

4 pork steaks

Year-Round Barbecue Rub
(page 277)

Dr. BBQ's Peachipotle
Barbecue Sauce (page
284)

My Canadian friends seem to love pork with fruit. It's usually pork loin with some berries, but I'm going to offer this simple recipe to them, which might be a little more Southern influenced. • **Yield: 4 servings**

Prepare the grill for direct cooking at medium heat, using peach wood for flavor. Apple will work if you can't find peach wood.

Season the steaks liberally with the rub. Put them on the grill and cook for about 10 minutes, then flip and cook another 10 minutes. Be careful not to burn them. If your grill is too hot, remove the steaks to a platter and cool it down.

When the steaks are almost done, brush with the barbecue sauce. Flip and brush the other side. Continue this process until you reach the degree of caramelization that you like.

Transfer to a platter. Tent loosely with foil and let rest 5 minutes.

King of the Q Grilled Pineapple Upside-Down Cake

A Recipe from Barbecue All Star Ted Reader

1 fresh pineapple

½ cup spiced rum

¼ cup butter

1 10-inch round cast-iron pan, 2 inches deep

½ cup packed brown sugar

1⅓ cups cake flour, sifted

2 teaspoons baking powder

¼ teaspoon salt

¾ cup sugar

¼ cup butter

1 large egg

½ cup whole milk

1 teaspoon vanilla extract

Ice cream or whipped cream for serving

Before I'd met him, Ted Reader was once described to me as "the Barbecue King of Canada." Well, he's definitely all that, but so much more. When you hang around with Ted in Canada he's constantly being greeted by fans and signing autographs. Ted has a few successful cookbooks and a very hot TV show called *King of the Q.* His sauce and seasoning line also carry that name. Ted is a very skilled chef and a wizard with flavors. He tastes things that most of us can't even imagine. I haven't tried it yet, but Ted tells me he smokes chocolate, and it's good. Hmmm. Ted Reader is a great guy and a good friend. When I asked him for a recipe for this book, I knew he'd give me something spectacular. I was right.

From Ted: "Grilled pineapple rules. It's the best fruit for grilling since it gets tender and really sweet when grilled. This recipe, of course, has rum and it just makes it even better. Have a blast and enjoy it upside down."

• **Yield: 8 servings**

Using a sharp knife, cut the top and bottom off the pineapple. Slice the rind away from the flesh of the pineapple. Cut out the eyes that remain from the rind. Cut the peeled pineapple into 1-inch-thick rounds. Core each round. Place the pineapple in a bowl and pour in the rum. Marinate the pineapple for 2 hours.

Preheat the grill for direct cooking at medium-high heat.

Remove the pineapple from the rum.   *continued*

Drink the flavored rum.

Grill the pineapple slices for 2 to 3 minutes per side until lightly charred. Remove from the grill and cool fully.

Preheat the oven to 350°F.

Over medium-low heat, melt the butter in the cast-iron pan. Add the brown sugar and stir until well blended. Remove from the heat. Arrange the pineapple on the sugar mixture. Set aside.

In a bowl, combine the cake flour, baking powder, salt, and sugar. Sift together three times and set aside.

In a mixer, cream the butter. Add the dry ingredients and the egg, milk, and vanilla. (If you have any leftover slices of grilled pineapple, then chop it coarsely and add to batter.) Stir to mix well and then beat on high for 1 to 2 minutes.

Pour the batter over the grilled pineapple in the cast-iron pan. Bake for 45 to 50 minutes, until the batter is cooked through. Cool the cake in the pan for 10 minutes. Invert onto a plate and let stand for 2 minutes.

Remove the pan. Serve with ice cream or whipped cream.

Independence Day:
A Fiery Fourth

▼▼

No, this is not the movie featuring a blown-up White House but rather an incendiary barbecue feast. Every U.S. citizen knows that the Fourth of July is the date that we celebrate the adoption of the Declaration of Independence, but not too many people know that many of the delegates to the Continental Congress were not even there to vote—the New York delegation did not vote until July 7, for example. But July 4 is the date that sticks, despite efforts to move it so there would be yet one more three-day goof-off weekend. But along with Christmas, New Year's, and Halloween, Independence Day is actually celebrated on its proper calendar day. The rest are mostly moved to convenient Mondays for department store sales, long weekends at Disney World and, in some states, the opening of fishing season.

We are celebrating the life of barbecue, liberty from the food police, and pursuit of happiness of indulgence during this holiday, and I have chosen, because of the fireworks, to make this menu mostly hot and spicy.

Grilled Hot Wings

Habanero Baby Back Ribs

Red, White, and Blue Potato Salad

Spice Cake on the Grill

▼▼▼▼▼

Grilled Hot Wings

4 pounds chicken wings

3 teaspoons ground cayenne pepper

2 teaspoons freshly ground black pepper

2 teaspoons onion powder

1 teaspoon dried thyme

1 teaspoon garlic powder

¼ teaspoon celery salt

Louisiana-style hot sauce

These wings are a tasty alternative to deep-frying the chicken. They're great as an appetizer for a summer barbecue. Put them on the grill before guests arrive so that their wonderful aroma greets them as they walk through the door. • **Yield: About 48 individual wings**

Note: This dish requires advance preparation.

Cut the tips off each wing and discard them or reserve them for another use, such as chicken stock. Using a sharp knife, separate the two remaining pieces at the joint.

Combine the cayenne, black pepper, onion, thyme, garlic, and celery salt in a large bowl. Add the wings to the bowl and turn them to evenly coat. Cover the bowl and refrigerate for 24 hours.

Oil the grill and prepare it for direct cooking at high heat. Turn off all but one burner and put the wings on the cooler part of the grill. Cover and cook until the chicken is done, about 45 minutes, or until the chicken juices run clear.

To serve, eat the the wings hot off the grill with the hot sauce served on the side.

Winter Solstice and Saturnalia
Craisined Pork Roast on a Plank, page 8

Carnival
Dr. BBQ's Barbecued Barbecue Shrimp (left), page 55

Super Bowl Barbecue
**Dr. BBQ's Wings with Pantry Sauce (above), page 48;
Rib Meat Potato Skins (below), page 49**

Saint Patrick's Day
**New World Smoked Corned Beef, page 81; Shamrock
Potatoes, page 82; Grilled Cabbage and Onions with Beer,
page 83; Irish Turnips and Carrots, page 84**

Easter
Smokin' Leg of Lamb (above), page 113

Cinco de Mayo
**The Perfect Margarita, page 127; Barbecue Enchilada Casserole
with Green Chile Barbecue Sauce, page 129**

Memorial Day (opposite)
Beefeater Martini, Straight Up, page 142; Grilled
Porterhouse Steaks, page 144

Willis Carrier's Birthday (above)
Smoked Cornish Hens, page 257; Linguine with
Cilantro and Parsley Pesto, page 259

Thanksgiving
The Ultimate Turkey, page 264;
Dr. BBQ's Pulled Pork Stuffing, page 265

Habanero Baby Back Ribs

2 slabs pork loin baby back ribs, about 4 pounds total

Peggy's Favorite Barbecue Rub (page 278)

1 cup habanero jelly, divided

¼ cup apple juice

I'm always looking for something new to do to ribs, and when I went to the Fiery Foods Show in Albuquerque, I met a few different people selling hot pepper jelly. I had a cookoff a week later in New Mexico, where I could take a chance with something spicy. So I got a really good jar of habanero jelly at the show from a company named Brimstone and I incorporated it in my rib recipe. I didn't win anything, but considering the spiciness of them an eleventh-place finish was very good. Not everybody likes barbecue this hot, but many of us do. • **Yield: 4 to 6 servings**

Prepare the grill or smoker for indirect cooking at 275°F, using hickory wood for flavor.

Remove the membrane from the bone side of the ribs. Wash the ribs in water to remove all the bone dust, and then pat dry with paper towels. Season the ribs liberally all over with the barbecue rub. Put the ribs on the cooker, meat side up. Cook for 1½ hours, then flip and cook for 30 minutes more.

Take the ribs off of the cooker and lay each on a big double-thick piece of aluminum foil. Spread each slab with ¼ cup of the jelly. Begin to close the foil up around the ribs, and add half of the apple juice to each packet. Wrap the ribs loosely but completely with the foil and set on the grill.

After 30 minutes, peek in the packet to make sure the liquid isn't all dried up. If it is, add a little more apple juice. Cook for about another 30 minutes, or until the ribs are tender.

Remove the ribs from the foil and return to the grill for 15 minutes to dry them out a bit.

Serve with the remaining jelly warm and on the side.

Red, White, and Blue Potato Salad

¾ pound baby blue or purple potatoes

¾ pound baby red potatoes

¾ pound baby white potatoes

¼ cup olive oil

1 teaspoon salt

½ teaspoon freshly ground white pepper

½ cup red wine vinegar

1 cup diced sweet white onion, Vidalia preferred

½ cup chopped scallions

1 cup chopped celery

½ cup chopped yellow or red bell peppers

3 tablespoons chopped Italian parsley

3 New Mexican green chiles, roasted, peeled, seeds and stems removed, and chopped (or substitute 4 yellow wax hots)

¾ cup red wine vinegar

¼ cup olive oil

½ teaspoon sugar

1 teaspoon minced basil

Here is the perfect potato salad for the Fourth of July, made with patriotic potatoes.

- **Yield: 8 to 10 servings**

Preheat the oven to 400°F.

Scrub the potatoes, but don't remove the skins. Put them in a large bowl, add the olive oil, and toss to coat the potatoes with the oil. Place the potatoes on a large cookie sheet and sprinkle with the salt and pepper. Spray the potatoes with a spritz of water. Cover the pan tightly with aluminum foil and roast for 30 to 35 minutes. Then test the doneness by piercing a few potatoes with a knife. The potatoes should be firm, not mushy.

Remove the potatoes from the oven, allow them to cool for a few minutes, and then cut them in half and place them in a large ceramic bowl.

Toss the potatoes with the vinegar, onion, scallions, celery, bell peppers, parsley, and chiles.

Mix together the vinegar, oil, and sugar in a small covered jar. Shake and pour over the potato-vegetable mixture. Toss the mixture, sprinkle the basil over the top, and serve.

Spice Cake on the Grill

2 cups all-purpose flour

½ cup sugar

1 teaspoon baking soda

1 cup milk

½ teaspoon ground anise

2 teaspoons rum

1 teaspoon ground cinnamon

2 tablespoons honey

½ cup blanched almond slivers

Yes, you can bake a cake on the grill. If you have any friends of French descent, they will be shocked, but once they taste it, they will praise you to the skies.

• **Yield: 6 to 8 servings**

Note: This recipe requires advance preparation.

In a bowl, combine the flour, sugar, baking soda, milk, anise, rum, and cinnamon. Mix with a wooden spoon until smooth. Cover and let stand at room temperature overnight. Stir in the honey and almonds.

Prepare the grill for indirect cooking at 350°F. Add the dough to a buttered loaf pan and cover with aluminum foil. Put on the grill and cook for 1¼ hours.

Unmold the cake when hot, but slice it and serve it when cold.

Bastille Day:
Barbecue Français

▼▼

When I was a kid and heard someone say the name of this holiday, I wondered why some country would have a day devoted to a stolen fish. Now I know that Bastille Day on July 14 is the French version of our Independence Day and the symbol of the end of the monarchy and the beginning of the French Republic.

On May 5, 1789, the king convened the Estates General to hear their complaints, but the assembly of the Third Estate, representing the citizens of Paris, soon broke away and formed the Constituent National Assembly. On June 20, 1789, the deputies of the Third Estate took the oath of the Jeu de Paume "to not separate until the Constitution has been established." The deputies' opposition was supported by public opinion. The people of Paris rose up and marched on the Bastille, a state prison that symbolized the power and control of the old regime.

The storming of the Bastille on July 14, 1789, was proof to the people that power no longer resided in the king or in God but in the people. On July 16, the king recognized the tricolor banner of the people, and the revolution had succeeded.

For all citizens of France, the storming of the Bastille symbolizes liberty, democracy, and the struggle against all forms of oppression.

To celebrate, the French hold an enormous military parade. There are many parties throughout the country with bands playing and people drinking. And, of course, there are the fireworks. My celebration menu explores a side of French partying that is not well known: grilling. But first, a toast to the French Revolution.

Bastille Cocktail

Grilled Tournedos with Madeira Sauce

Grilled Tuna and Garlic with Quick Piperade Sauce

Potato Gratin with Blue Cheese

Black Pepper Strawberries

▼▼▼▼

Bastille Cocktail

1 ounce cognac

½ ounce freshly squeezed lemon juice

1 teaspoon bar sugar

3 ounces chilled champagne

Lemon twist for garnish

Let them drink cognac and champagne—in the same glass! • **Yield: 1 serving**

In a shaker, combine the cognac, lemon juice, and sugar with crushed ice and shake well. Strain into a fluted champagne glass. Top with champagne. Garnish with the lemon twist, if desired.

Grilled Tournedos with Madeira Sauce

2 tablespoons butter

2 medium carrots, diced

1 medium onion, chopped

2 sprigs parsley

Pinch of thyme

1 small bay leaf

2 tablespoons all-purpose flour

1 cup dry white wine

1½ cups beef stock

1 tablespoon tomato paste

Salt and freshly ground black pepper to taste

2 tablespoons chopped mushrooms

¼ cup Madeira wine, or substitute port

6 tournedos of beef

½ cup softened butter

Tournedos are deluxe steaks that are cut from the most tender section of the fillet. It is a round cut, about 2 inches across and 1 inch thick. It is cooked rare or medium rare—never well done. • **Yield: 6 servings**

To make the sauce, heat the butter in a saucepan and add the carrots, onion, parsley, thyme, and bay leaf. Cook over low heat, stirring constantly, until the vegetables are golden brown. Stir in the flour and cook until lightly brown. Add the wine, beef stock, tomato paste, and salt and pepper and bring to a boil. Reduce the heat and simmer, covered, for 30 minutes. Strain into another saucepan, add the mushrooms and Madeira, and simmer for 5 minutes.

To make the tournedos, prepare the grill for direct cooking at medium-high heat. Using a knife, spread the butter on both sides of the tournedos. Place them on the grill and cook for about 3 minutes per side, or until medium rare.

To serve, place some sauce on a plate, add a tournedos, and place a little sauce on top.

Grilled Tuna and Garlic with Quick Piperade Sauce

3 tablespoons olive oil

1 red bell pepper, seeds and stems removed, chopped

1 medium onion, chopped

3 cloves garlic, minced

One 14.5-ounce can diced or stewed tomatoes

1 tablespoon hot sauce of choice, or more to taste

4 tuna steaks, rinsed and patted dry

2 tablespoons olive oil

Salt and freshly ground black pepper to taste

This is a recipe from the Basque region of France, where they love fish. They also love spicy sauces, as indicated by this recipe and the fact that this dish is frequently seen on the menus of bistros in the region.

• **Yield: 4 servings**

To make the sauce, add the olive oil to a medium skillet and heat. Add the bell pepper, onion, and garlic and sauté until they are soft. Add the tomatoes, stir, cover, and cook over low heat for 15 minutes. Uncover, add the hot sauce, and simmer until slightly thickened.

To make the tuna, prepare the grill for direct cooking at high heat. Brush the steaks with olive oil and sprinkle with salt and pepper. Grill for about 5 minutes per side; the steaks should be pink in the middle. Remove to individual plates and top with the Piperade Sauce.

Potato Gratin with Blue Cheese

3 cups whole milk

½ cup crumbled blue cheese

½ cup light cream

4 tablespoons butter

2 pounds potatoes, peeled and thinly sliced

Freshly grated nutmeg

Salt and freshly ground black pepper to taste

Here is another one of those simple dishes that tastes so great. The inspiration is from the Auvergne region in central France, where they make many varieties of blue-veined cow's milk cheeses. • **Yield: 6 servings**

Preheat the oven to 375°F. Add the milk to a saucepan and scald it. Combine the blue cheese and the cream in a blender and process until smooth.

Coat a shallow baking dish with some of the butter. Add half the potatoes to the dish and season with nutmeg and salt and pepper. Add half of the cheese-cream mixture. Layer the remaining potatoes and season with nutmeg, salt, and pepper. Add the remaining cheese-cream mixture, the milk, and top with the remaining butter.

Bake uncovered for about 1½ hours, until the top is crisp and golden.

Black Pepper Strawberries

2 pints strawberries, washed and hulled

3 teaspoons freshly squeezed lemon juice

¼ cup freshly squeezed orange juice

3 tablespoons sugar

1½ teaspoons freshly ground black pepper

During strawberry season in Europe, this dessert can be found in many restaurants. It is an unusual combination of ingredients, and if you're feeling decadent, top the berries with a dollop of sweetened whipped cream.

• **Yield: 6 to 8 servings**

Place the drained berries in a large bowl and sprinkle the top with the remaining ingredients.

Toss gently to coat and marinate the berries for 1 hour in the refrigerator.

Spoon into stemmed glasses and serve.

Dog Days of Summer:
Featuring Various "Hot Dogs"

▼▼

Variously known as the "dog days" or "summer doldrums," the month of August seems to have nothing going for it. We're going to do something about that by proclaiming the third Sunday in August to be Dog Day. This is the day when all grills and smokers are devoted to the various sausages that are known as hot dogs. And I've spiced them up a bit so that you'll know that they're hot in more than one way.

Some people are into grinding and spicing their meats, stuffing their casings, and creating their own sausages and I say, buy a book on sausage making and have at it. I think that most delis have a really good selection of sausages such as bratwurst, knockwurst, Italian sausage, and those great Hebrew National hot dogs, so I just buy those. I do like to make some homemade condiments, though. Here are a few choices for your Dog Day celebration.

Old-Fashioned Lemonade

Mini Dogs in Beer and Barbecue Sauce

Brats on the Barbie with the Spiciest Mustard

Dr. BBQ's Chili Dogs

Yams, Bananas, and Habs

White Chocolate Ancho Chile Ice Cream

▼▼▼▼▼

Old-Fashioned Lemonade

1½ cups sugar

1½ cups water

1 tablespoon freshly
grated lemon zest

Juice of 7 lemons

1 lemon, sliced thinly

Mint sprigs for garnish

There are an infinite number of variations on lemonade, but I decided that once people had the basic recipe, they could add whatever else they wanted, like vodka. • **Yield: 10 servings**

In small saucepan, stir together the sugar, water, and lemon zest. Bring to a boil, stirring constantly; boil for 5 minutes, stirring. Remove from the heat and let cool. Stir in the lemon juice.

Transfer to a jar; cover and refrigerate for up to 3 weeks. To serve, place 2 ice cubes in each tall glass. Add ¼ cup of the syrup and ¾ cup cold water and stir well.

Garnish with a lemon slice and sprig of mint.

Mini Dogs in Beer and Barbecue Sauce

36 mini hot dogs

2 cups Dr. BBQ's
Peachipotle Barbecue
Sauce (page 284)

1 cup beer

These may not be haute cuisine, but they sure are good. Let he who has not eaten a mini dog cast the first stone. • **Yield: 6 to 8 servings**

Prepare the cooker for indirect cooking at 325°F, using peach or apple wood for flavor.

Put the mini dogs in an aluminum foil pan. Mix the barbecue sauce and the beer, and pour over the dogs. Toss to coat evenly.

Place the pan in the cooker and cook for 1½ hours.

Brats on the Barbie
with the Spiciest Mustard

Two 12-ounce bottles of beer of choice

1 onion, chopped

8 bratwursts

8 buns

Hot Horseradish Mustard (page 289)

Brats are a religion in Wisconsin, where I've had them many times. This is the classic beer treatment, and I've added a recipe for a very hot homemade mustard.

• **Yield: 8 servings**

To prepare the brats, add the beer and onion to a large pot. Bring the beer to a simmer and add the brats. Simmer (do *not* boil) for 20 minutes.

Prepare the grill for direct cooking at high heat. Place the brats on the grill and grill them for about 15 minutes, turning often with tongs.

To serve, place the brats in the buns and slather with the mustard.

Dr. BBQ's Chili Dogs

8 Hebrew National hot dogs

8 hot dog buns

Dr. BBQ's Hot Dog Sauce (page 287)

These are the traditional chili dogs that have been served in New York for decades, except I grill them. They are sloppy but delicious. • **Yield: 8 servings**

Prepare the grill for direct cooking at high heat. Place the dogs on the grate and grill them for about 15 minutes, turning often with tongs.

To assemble, place the dogs in the buns and top with the sauce.

Yams, Bananas, and Habs

4 medium yams, peeled and quartered

2 tablespoons olive oil

1 medium onion, chopped

2 cloves garlic, crushed

1 habanero chile, seeded, deveined, and minced (you may want to use only ½ of the habanero because they are very hot)

4 large bananas, peeled and sliced

4 tablespoons butter, cut into small pieces

1 tablespoon salt

1 teaspoon coarsely ground black pepper

This idea comes from an old island recipe. I added the habanero because the taste was just a little flat without it. There's no such thing as a flat dish with habanero. Be very careful when handling habaneros. I wear rubber gloves. • **Yield: 6 to 8 servings**

Prepare the cooker for indirect cooking at 325°F, using apple wood for flavor.

In a kettle of boiling salted water, cook the yams until tender, about 15 minutes. Drain and reserve.

In a big skillet over medium heat, add the oil. When it's hot, add the onion and sauté for about 5 minutes, or until soft. Add the garlic and the habanero and cook for 2 minutes. Add the bananas and cook for 3 minutes.

Add the yams, butter, salt and pepper. Toss everything well to coat. Cook for another 5 minutes, mashing the yams and bananas and mixing everything together.

Transfer to a foil pan. Place in the cooker for 1 hour. Remove and serve.

White Chocolate Ancho Chile Ice Cream

3 ancho chiles, stems removed

½ teaspoon ground cinnamon

¼ teaspoon ground cloves

6 ounces (2 bars) good quality white chocolate such as Tobler or Lindt

2 cups heavy cream

2 cups milk

¾ cup sugar

1 vanilla bean

6 egg yolks

Chile peppers in ice cream? Well, the anchos are quite mild and they have a raisiny aroma and flavor, so this treat really works. • **Yield: 1 quart**

Note: This recipe requires advance preparation.

Cover the chiles with hot water and let soak for 15 minutes or until pliable. Remove the chiles and discard most of the seeds. Place in a blender or food processor and puree until smooth. Use a little of the soaking water if necessary. Stir in the cinnamon and cloves.

Melt the chocolate in a double boiler over hot water.

Combine the cream, milk, and sugar. Split the vanilla bean and scrape some of the seeds into the mixture. Bring to a boil.

While whisking the egg yolks, pour in about ⅓ of the hot milk mixture. Reheat the remaining milk and add the egg yolks. Heat for 1 minute, whisking constantly.

Strain the mixture into a bowl. Stir in the chiles and chocolate and chill.

Freeze in an ice-cream maker according to the manufacturer's directions.

Labor Day:
The Heartland Grill

▼▼

The official end of summer is Labor Day, the first Monday in September. No matter that summer actually ends September 21, on the autumnal equinox: Labor Day is the end of summer because we go back to work after months of vacation. Well, months of summer partying anyway.

Grilling on Labor Day begs an interesting question. Is grilling working? Do you say, "That's too much work and this is Labor Day, a day of no work, so I'm not going to grill." I would reply that grilling is not work, it is sheer pleasure and creativity all rolled into one. Maybe you can get your significant other to do the grilling, and you can lie in the hammock. But I am still confused by the concept of celebrating work by not working. That's like celebrating laziness by working your tail off.

Dangerous Slush

Grilled Iowa Pork Chops

Grown-Up Tater Tots

Slow-Cooker Homemade Applesauce

Broccoli Slaw

All-American Apple Pie

▼▼▼▼

Dangerous Slush

1 large can frozen orange juice concentrate

1 large can frozen lemonade concentrate

1 large can frozen limeade concentrate

1 large bag frozen strawberries

1 fifth decent-quality tequila

We all know that driving in slush can be dangerous, and drinking this slush with unbridled abandon can be dangerous, too. It can be served before the meal or even as a highly potent frozen dessert to cool down those taste buds. • **Yield: 10 to 15 servings, depending on imbibing habits and whether or not it is used as a dessert**

Note: This recipe requires advance preparation.

Pour all of the ingredients into a plastic 1-gallon container and shake to mix. Then add enough water to come up to within 2 inches of the top. Shake the container again.

Seal the container tightly and freeze overnight.

Cut a 3- to 4-inch area open at the top of the container and scoop the slush into dessert glasses. Serve with a spoon, followed by a straw when the mixture starts to melt.

Grilled Iowa Pork Chops

4 Iowa chops

2 tablespoons olive oil

Dr. BBQ's Pork Seasoning
(page 281)

My good friend Anne Rehnstrom, from the Pork Board in Des Moines, tells me that there really is a cut called an Iowa chop. There really is a Pork Board, too, and they are big supporters of all things barbecue. The specifications for the Iowa chop are very simple. It has to be a bone-in, center-cut loin chop, cut between 1¼ and 1½ inches thick. That sounds just about right to me. It would be a shame to do anything but grill a beautiful cut like that.

• **Yield:** 4 servings

Prepare the grill for direct cooking at medium-high heat, using apple wood for flavor.

Brush the chops all over with the olive oil, then season them liberally on both sides with the seasoning.

Put the chops directly on the grill. Cook for 5 to 7 minutes per side, or until golden brown and at an internal temp of 145°F. (The USDA would like you to cook them to 160°F. Your choice.) Remove to a platter and serve.

Grown-Up Tater Tots

2 medium potatoes, peeled and diced

3 tablespoons finely chopped onions

½ cup coarsely grated Parmesan cheese

2 tablespoons chopped fresh parsley

1 large egg, lightly beaten

Salt to taste

Vegetable oil for frying

Remember those tater tots from the school cafeteria? Here is a grown-up version. They go great with the homemade applesauce. I like to rinse the onions to mellow them out a bit, because these potatoes don't cook long enough to remove the sharpness of raw onions.

• **Yield: 4 servings**

Put the potatoes in a saucepan, cover with water, and cook until tender. Remove, drain, and place in a bowl. Roughly mash the potatoes, using a fork, so that they still have some texture.

Place the onions in a strainer and hold under cold running water for 1 minute to remove any bitterness. Drain well and add to the potatoes. Add all the remaining ingredients except the oil, and lightly toss to mix, using a couple of forks or even your hands to prevent the potatoes from breaking down. They need to retain some of the lumps and texture.

Heat a heavy, wide skillet over medium-high heat, add the oil to a depth of ¼ inch, and when hot, drop the potato mixture by the heaping tablespoon into the pan. Gently press with a spatula to form little cakes. Fry until brown on one side, turn once, and brown on the other side.

Slow-Cooker Homemade Applesauce

4 large apples, peeled, cored, and sliced (Granny Smith recommended)

½ cup brown sugar, packed

1½ tablespoons freshly squeezed lemon juice

1 teaspoon ground cinnamon

This is one of the easiest applesauce recipes that I've ever made. Just toss everything in the slow cooker early in the day and it'll be ready for dinnertime.

• **Yield: 3 cups**

In your slow cooker, combine the apples, brown sugar, and lemon juice and stir well. Cook, covered, on high for 3 to 4 hours.

Mash with a potato masher into the consistency you desire. Stir in the cinnamon and mix well.

Broccoli Slaw

⅓ cup orange juice

⅓ cup vinegar

2 teaspoons minced shallots

Coarse salt to taste

1 tablespoon sesame oil

1 tablespoon grated ginger

1 teaspoon yellow mustard

One 10-ounce bag broccoli slaw

A package of broccoli slaw can be found in the produce section of just about any supermarket. It can be made into many different things, but this is my favorite. • **Yield: 4 servings**

In a bowl, combine the orange juice, vinegar, and shallots. Add a good pinch of salt. Let this stand 5 to 20 minutes, as long as you can.

Whisk in the sesame oil, ginger, and mustard. Taste and adjust seasonings. Add the broccoli slaw to the bowl and toss to combine.

Serve immediately.

All-American Apple Pie

8 cups peeled, cored, and sliced apples

½ cup firmly packed light brown sugar

1 tablespoon freshly squeezed lemon juice

½ teaspoon ground cinnamon

¼ teaspoon ground nutmeg

⅓ cup sugar

¾ cup all-purpose flour

6 tablespoons butter

1 commercial prepared pie shell

2 tablespoons cold unsalted butter, cut into little pieces

What a fitting ending for Labor Day, a true American classic. Do I eat two pieces? You bet. Do I eat them with vanilla ice cream? No, I eat them with chocolate chip ice cream.

• **Yield: 8 servings (6 if I am at the party)**

Preheat the oven to 400°F.

Combine the apples, brown sugar, lemon juice, cinnamon, and nutmeg in a large mixing bowl; toss well to mix. Set aside.

To make the topping, mix the sugar with the flower in a bowl; then cut in the butter with a pastry knife until the mixture is crumbly.

Place the apple mixture in the pie shell, scatter the 2 tablespoons butter over it, and sprinkle the topping over it. Bake for 40 minutes. Remove from the oven and allow to cool to room temperature before serving.

Fall

▼▼▼▼▼▼▼▼▼▼▼

A Bountiful Time
for Barbecue

Back to School Barbecue:
A Lunch for Kids

Patsy Cline's Birthday:
A Barbecue Tribute

Jack Daniel's Birthday:
An Old Barbecue Tradition

Columbus Day:
Italian Festival Grill

Eggtoberfest:
A Great Barbecue Event

Halloween:
Pumpkin Grill and More

Melbourne Cup Day:
Barbecue in Australia

Football Tailgating:
Yet More Portable Grilling

Willis Carrier's Birthday:
A Barbecue Salute to the Father of Cool

Thanksgiving:
The Ultimate Turkey and More

realize that for most people summer is the peak of barbecue and that after you throw a few of my favorite summer barbecue parties you may think you've had your fill. But once you see the autumn menus and recipes I've come up with you'll surely change your mind.

Fall has always been my favorite season. It is a time of change in most parts of the country. I grew up in Chicago, where fall was a last gasp of warm weather before the long, hard winter to come. Now I live in Florida, where half of autumn takes place during hurricane season, but that never stops us from barbecuing. Matter of fact, the hurricanes regularly blow down the power lines so everyone has to cook on the grill because the stove won't work. Enough about the weather. Enjoy the warm days and cool nights for grilling and smoking.

One thing I really enjoy in the fall is the nonstop football. In my humble opinion it is the best sport, with the possible exception of NASCAR. We do refer to barbecue cookoffs as a sport, but even I can't make a fair comparison between that and football. There are two kinds of sports. The first is where the fans can have a few beers, and the second is where the participants (athletes?) can have a

few beers. Bowling and golf come to mind as well as barbecue cooking.

I really like a football-barbecue day when you keep the TV next to the cooker (but not *too* close). I can then spend the day doing two things I really enjoy. I plan the cooking around all the critical parts of the game. Get all the prep done before the game starts. For a grilling menu, watch the beginning; when things slow down, get the grill lit. Cook during halftime, eat during the third quarter, and be back in the comfy chair for the exciting finish. What a plan! If you're cooking some slow-cooked barbecue, you can have all the work done in the morning, and if you time it right, the food will be ready for you at halftime. I have not accounted for doubleheaders, or even triple-headers. It can be a long day when your team is playing the evening game. You'll definitely need to pace your beer consumption on those days.

There was a time when I thought that fall was a good time to batten down the hatches for winter hibernation, but then I suddenly realized that I don't hibernate during the winter. I barbecue (see Part 1), so I'm back to my old "any excuse for a barbecue" philosophy. Following are my favorite reasons for a fall barbecue.

Back to School Barbecue:
A Lunch for Kids

▼▼

Back to school is an exciting time of year for kids. I don't have any great culinary stories from when I was a kid, unless you count the time I sat at the dinner table for two hours because I wouldn't eat some spinach, but I do have a story about the beginning of my literary career. I was about ten years old, and the English teacher gave us an assignment to write a story and paint a picture to go along with the story. I came up with a great idea and got right on it. My story was about "The First Polack on the Moon." You see, when I was growing up in the '60s, political correctness hadn't become popular, and people were comfortable kidding about their heritage. My mom was all French, and my dad was German and Polish. The German part of the family was gone, so my dad regularly referred to himself and his relatives as Polacks. There was no harm meant at all, and he was proud of his heritage. So anyway, I painted a picture of a guy standing on the moon with a Polish flag, and I wrote a story about this heroic Polish astronaut named Wadick, who was "The First Polack on the Moon." Believe me, I didn't think this was funny at all and I wasn't trying to insult anyone. I thought I had written a great story with a great picture because I was proud of my Polish heritage. I fully expected my grade to be an A. Imagine my surprise when I got my paper back and I had a failing grade and a note to my parents that they needed to come in for a conference. I guess maybe I helped invent political correctness, because the teacher thought it was inappropriate that I wrote and spoke like that. I guess that adds one more teacher to the list who would be surprised about how things have turned out for me.

The menu has nothing to do with the story, but I've been meaning to tell that one for a while now. The menu is about making good food for brown-bag lunches. These are fine for Mom and Dad, too. Just remember this: When you send any member of your family off with a packed lunch, send it in one of those thermal containers that will keep the food cold until lunchtime. Otherwise, you might get a call from, say, the school nurse just about four hours after lunch. My idea is to make your own lunch meat substitute. It's cheaper than most lunch meat, tastes better, and is definitely better for you.

Smoked Pork Loin Sandwiches with
Dave's Homemade Honey Mustard

Grilled Fruit Cocktail

Chocolate Chunk Pecan Cookies

▼▼▼▼

Smoked Pork Loin Sandwiches with Dave's Homemade Honey Mustard

1 boneless pork roast (3 to 4 pounds)

Peggy's Favorite Barbecue Rub (page 278)

Hamburger buns

Leaves of romaine lettuce, washed

Slices of tomato

Dave's Homemade Honey Mustard (page 288)

I like to smoke a pork loin on Sunday and serve it cold and sliced for lunch all week. • **Yield 8 to 12 sandwiches**

Note: This recipe requires advance preparation.

Prepare the cooker for indirect cooking at 250°F, using apple wood for flavor.

Season the pork liberally with the rub. Put the pork roast in the cooker, fat side up. Cook until the pork reaches an internal temp of 145°F. (The USDA would recommend 160°F.) Remove to a platter. Let rest for 15 minutes. Wrap tightly in aluminum foil and refrigerate for at least 4 hours, but preferably overnight.

After the pork is thoroughly cooled, slice it thinly by hand, cutting only what you need at a time.

To make the sandwiches, spread a layer of the mustard on the bottom of the bun, top with a healthy portion of pork, a leaf of lettuce, a slice of tomato, and the top of the bun.

Grilled Fruit Cocktail

1 pineapple, peeled, cored, and cut into spears

6 kiwi, halved

20 seedless grapes, on skewers

12 strawberries, on skewers

2 pears, peeled, cored, and quartered

2 apples, peeled, cored, and quartered

2 to 3 tablespoons honey

This grilled fruit cocktail is a winner.
• Yield: 6 to 8 servings

Prepare the grill for direct cooking at high heat.

One by one, grill the fruits just for a few minutes each. You really don't want to cook any of it, you simply want to impart a grill flavor, and brown them a little. As the fruits are done remove them to a platter.

Place the grapes in a bowl. Cut the rest of the fruit into bite-size pieces and add them to the bowl. Drizzle the whole bowl of fruit with the honey and toss gently. Add a little more honey if you wish.

Cover the bowl and refrigerate. To send off with the bag lunch, spoon the fruit into a small sealed bowl. And don't forget to send a fork.

Chocolate Chunk Pecan Cookies

½ pound unsalted butter

1 cup light brown sugar

¾ cup sugar

2 eggs, beaten

1 tablespoon vanilla

2½ cups all-purpose flour

½ teaspoon salt

½ teaspoon baking powder

½ teaspoon baking soda

3 cups chocolate chunks

1 cup chopped pecans

What kid can resist cookies loaded with chocolate? Mrs. Fields, move over, Dr. BBQ is taking over the cookie detail. • **Yield: About 3 dozen cookies**

Preheat the oven to 375°F.

In a large mixing bowl, combine the butter, brown sugar, sugar, eggs, and vanilla and cream with an electric mixer.

In a separate bowl, sift the flour, salt, baking powder, and baking soda. When combined, gradually add the flour mixture to the batter and beat until just combined and smooth.

Next, add the chocolate chunks and nuts.

Scoop the cookies onto a greased cookie sheet, using a generous tablespoon for each, and bake until light golden brown, or about 10 minutes.

Remove from the cookie sheet while hot. Serve with milk.

Patsy Cline's Birthday:
A Barbecue Tribute

▼▼▼

One of the most famous—and tragic—singers in country music history was born on September 8, 1932. Her birth certificate is available for viewing online at *Patsified.com*. She had an amazing and unique way of singing a song. Patsy rose to the top of the country and pop charts with such hits as "Crazy" (written by Willie Nelson), "I Fall to Pieces," and "Faded Love." At the young age of thirty, she died in a plane crash.

Nowadays, Patsy Cline is immortalized by karaoke singers worldwide. I wonder how she'd feel about that? I can't verify Patsy Cline's love of barbecue, but since she was a good country girl I'd bet on it. This barbecue is dedicated to her memory.

All-Star BBQ Showdown Beef Brisket

Crazy French Fries

Sweet Dreams Potato Pie

▼▼▼▼

All-Star BBQ Showdown Beef Brisket

In 2005, I had the pleasure of being part of the first season of *All-Star BBQ Showdown* on the Outdoor Life Network. They put together a great concept: the cooks don't know what they'll be cooking, or what grill or smoker they'll be cooking on, until the last minute. I assure you it's nerve-racking. We are allowed to bring one ingredient with us, and our knives. I guessed that we would be cooking briskets because we were in Texas, so I brought my secret brisket injection. It's called Fab B, and is only available through www.theingredientstore.com. This stuff is just amazing. It makes the briskets plump up like nothing I've ever seen, and it makes them taste really beefy. I highly recommend it.

My first episode was filmed in Texas, and I was pitted against Myron Mixon from Vienna, Georgia, and Randy Pauly from Houston, Texas. These two guys have both won world championships, and Myron has won more grand championships than anyone anywhere. If you were discussing the best barbecue contest guys of all time, his name would be on the very short list. On this day we were given big whole briskets, and a very nice Oklahoma-style offset cooker from Horizon Smokers. I am very proud to have won that day. I got a nice trophy and a giant check for $3,000. Here's exactly what I did. • **Yield: About 10 servings**

Note: This recipe requires advance preparation.

5 ounces by measure of Fab B (only available at www.theingredientstore.com)

10 ounces water

¼ teaspoon cayenne pepper

Peggy's Favorite Barbecue Rub (page 278)

One 12-pound USDA Choice whole brisket, untrimmed

½ cup Big Bob Gibson's Championship Red Sauce*

½ cup Big Bob Gibson's Habanero Barbecue Sauce*

2 tablespoons honey

2 tablespoons apple jelly

*Available at www.Hawgeyesbbq.com

At least 8 hours before you plan to cook, combine the Fab B, the water, and the cayenne and mix thoroughly. Do not refrigerate. Exactly 4 hours before you plan to cook, inject the mixture evenly throughout the whole brisket. Apply a heavy coating of Peggy's Favorite Rub. Return the brisket to the refrigerator to rest for 4 hours.

Prepare the cooker for indirect cooking at 225°F, using pecan wood for flavor. Put the brisket on the cooker, fat side down. Cook slowly for 8 hours. Then you can raise the temp to 250°F. Continue cooking until the brisket reaches an internal temp of 180°F.

Wrap the brisket in a double layer of heavy-duty aluminum foil, now switching to fat side up. Return to the cooker until the brisket reaches an internal temp of 195°F. Remove to an empty ice chest and let rest for 2 hours. This whole process will take about 12 hours, but be sure to check the temps to get it just right.

Meanwhile, combine the 2 barbecue sauces with the honey and jelly and bring to a simmer to blend. Remove from heat.

Take the brisket out of the ice chest. Be very careful because there will be hot liquid accumulated in the foil. Reserve ¼ cup of the liquid and add it to the barbecue sauce mixture.

Unwrap the brisket and remove all the outside fat. Separate the point from the flat. The point is the odd-shaped muscle right under the fat cap. Cut the point into cubes and toss with a little of the sauce. These are "burnt ends" and should be served as a second dish alongside the sliced brisket.

Slice the flat muscle and brush each slice lightly with the sauce mixture before serving.

Crazy French Fries

4 large baking potatoes, peeled, rinsed, and patted dry

Vegetable oil cooking spray

2 egg whites

1 tablespoon Big-Time BBQ Rub (page 279)

T hese fries taste better than deep-fried ones, even though they have almost no fat.

• **Yield: 4 to 6 servings**

Preheat the oven to 400°F.

Cut the potatoes lengthwise until you render them into sticks ¼ inch wide on each side.

Spray the vegetable spray liberally on a baking sheet.

In a large bowl, mix together the egg whites and the rub. Add the potato sticks and stir to coat them well. Remove them from the bowl and place on the baking sheet in a single layer.

Bake for about 45 minutes, turning them every 10 minutes with a spatula.

Sweet Dreams Potato Pie

The Crust

1½ cups all-purpose flour

1 cup chopped pecans

½ cup butter, melted

2 tablespoons sugar

The Filling

¼ cup butter, softened

1 cup sugar

2 eggs, separated

1½ cups cooked and mashed sweet potatoes

¾ cup evaporated milk or half-and-half

1 teaspoon vanilla extract

½ teaspoon ground cinnamon

½ teaspoon ground nutmeg

¼ teaspoon ground ginger

Whipped cream for serving

It's amazing to me that something like sweet potatoes make such a tasty pie. This is a great finish to anything barbecued or grilled. If you want to substitute pumpkin for the sweet potatoes, I will not track you down and hurt you.

• Yield: 8 servings

Preheat the oven to 350°F.

To make the crust, combine the ingredients in a bowl and press into the bottom and sides of a 9 × 13-inch pan. Bake for 10 minutes, or until it turns a light golden color. Let cool.

To make the filling, cream the butter in a bowl with a mixer. Gradually add ¾ cup of the sugar and beat well. Beat in the egg yolks. Stir in the sweet potatoes, milk, vanilla, cinnamon, nutmeg, and ginger and mix well.

Beat the egg whites until foamy. Gradually add the remaining ¼ cup sugar, 1 tablespoon at a time, and beat until peaks form. Fold into the sweet potato mixture. Pour into the cooled pie shell and bake for 40 to 45 minutes.

Let cool and top with whipped cream.

Jack Daniel's Birthday:
An Old Barbecue Tradition

▼▼

Jack Daniel's, the company, is a good friend to the barbecue community. They support events around the country, and they hold the Jack Daniel's World Championship Invitational Barbecue for us every October. They also make the great whiskey that so many of us drink while cooking. If you've never paid a visit to Lynchburg, Tennessee, you really should. The people are as nice and genuine as you could possibly imagine. The old town square is full of stores that sell cool Jack Daniel's merchandise. Last time I was there they were even selling my books. There's a really neat store there that sells furniture and stuff made from discarded whiskey barrels. You can catch a horse and carriage ride up to Mr. Jack's grave, too. It's the one with the two chairs in front of the headstone. The chairs are said to be there for the local ladies who are still mourning his passing. I like to think of Lynchburg, Tennessee, as Disney for adults, with whiskey instead of a mouse.

Many of the locals from Lynchburg have become very involved in the barbecue cookoff circuit. David Roper is a Jack Daniel's distillery tour guide, barbecue judge, and legendary barbecue consumer. Phillip and Kathy Brazier are well known around Lynchburg, as well as around the cookoff circuit. Marsha Russell, who appears in many places in my books, has family ties to the distillery that go way back, and she cooks with John Hale, who works in the office and is actually a first cousin, three times removed, to Mr. Jack himself.

On my recent visit to Lynchburg, Marsha took me to meet local historian Roger Brashears. Roger tells me that Mr. Jack was born in September, but that nobody really knows the actual date. They see this as a positive, as it's an excuse to hold a monthlong birthday party. See why we like these guys? Well, I'm good with that, so happy birthday, Mr. Jack. I'll be celebrating all month long.

Cubby's Sinful Sausage Dip

Whiskey Pork Chops

Tennessee Hoe Cakes

Chocolate Whiskey Balls

▼▼▼▼

Cubby's Sinful Sausage Dip

A Recipe from Barbecue All Star John Hale

Two 16-ounce loaves of French bread

One 8-ounce package cream cheese, softened

One 8-ounce tub sour cream

2 cups shredded cheddar cheese

1 cup smoked sausage, chopped

⅓ cup chopped green onions

⅓ cup chopped green bell pepper

¼ teaspoon Worcestershire sauce

¼ teaspoon garlic powder

Paprika

This recipe comes from John Hale, aka Cubby. Not only is John a Barbecue All Star, he's kin to Jack Daniel. John cooked on the Jack Daniel's Barbecue Team for years before it was disbanded. They had a cooker built to look like a bottle of whiskey. In his real job, John is a buyer for the Jack Daniel's parent company, but on weekends you'll find him cooking barbecue somewhere. Usually it's with Marsha as the Late Night Whiskey Smokers. They do very well and always have a good time. I'll cook next to them anytime.

• **Yield: Serves many as an appetizer**

Preheat the oven or cooker to 350°F. Slice off the top fourth of 1 bread loaf and hollow out the bottom section, leaving a 1-inch shell.

Cut the bread top, inside pieces, and the second loaf into 1-inch cubes. Place the bread shell and cubes on a large baking sheet.

Bake for 12 minutes or until brown. Remove from the oven. Cover the cubes and reserve them. Meanwhile beat the cream cheese at medium speed until smooth, Add the sour cream, beating until creamy. Stir in the cheddar cheese, sausage, green onions, pepper, Worcestershire, and garlic powder.

Spoon the cheese mixture into the bread shell, wrap it in aluminum foil and place it on a baking sheet.

Cook the bread shell at 350°F for 30 minutes; unwrap it and place on a platter. Sprinkle with paprika. Serve with reserved cubes for dipping.

Whiskey Pork Chops

4 bone-in center-cut pork
chops, 1¼ inches thick

Ray's Whiskey Marinade
(page 293)

Barbecue sauce for
serving

Grillers must always be concerned with the proximity of their whiskey to the fire. After all, it is flammable.

- **Yield: 4 servings**

Note: This recipe requires advance preparation.

The night before you plan to cook, put the pork chops in a large zip bag. Pour the marinade over them. Squeeze the air out of the bag and refrigerate overnight.

Prepare the grill for cooking at high heat, using pecan wood for flavor. Take the chops out of the bag and put them directly on the grill. After 2 minutes, rotate (don't turn) the chops. This helps make those nice crosshatch grill marks. Cook another 3 minutes, or until the bottom is nicely browned, and flip.

Cook until the internal temp reaches 145°F. This should take about another 5 minutes. I must tell you that the Pork Board recommends cooking pork to 160°F, but I don't.

Remove the chops to a platter, tent loosely with foil, and let them rest for 5 minutes. Serve with barbecue sauce on the side.

Tennessee Hoe Cakes

1½ cups cornmeal

½ cup self-rising flour

½ teaspoon salt

½ cup milk

½ cup water

½ cup finely chopped onion (optional)

Butter for serving

These are so named because they were originally cooked on the flat blade of a hoe over hot coals, or so the story goes. Wouldn't a shovel work better? These cakes are often served with barbecue, especially in Tennessee.

• **Yield: About 12 cakes**

Combine all ingredients in a bowl and mix to a pancakelike batter. Drop by tablespoons on a hot greased griddle or frying pan. (Keep each cake small enough to turn easily.)

Cook as you would pancakes, turning only once. Serve hot with butter.

Chocolate Whiskey Balls

½ cup softened butter

2 pounds confectioner's sugar

1 cup Tennessee whiskey

1 cup finely chopped pecans or walnuts

6 ounces very good dark chocolate (I like Noir Special from Frey chocolates of Switzerland)

I think you know which brand of whiskey I'm going to use. **Yield: 8 or more servings**

In a bowl, cream together the butter and sugar, gradually adding the whiskey. Add the pecans and form into balls. Refrigerate 1 hour until firm.

Melt the chocolate in a double boiler, and using tongs, dip the balls into chocolate until covered. Put the balls on waxed paper to cool and refrigerate them to set the chocolate.

Columbus Day:
Italian Festival Grill

▼▼

This is a controversial subject because, based on the work of a lot of contemporary historians, Columbus is charged with trafficking in slaves, murder, spreading disease, and not even really discovering America in the first place. Now, I've been known to associate with some scoundrels and thieves in my life, so it's hard for me to cast the first stone in anyone's direction. While I don't condone any of the bad stuff Columbus might have done, those of us who barbecue owe him a culinary debt. For us, the reason to celebrate this historic day with a barbecue is that Columbus was the first European to discover chile peppers, and he brought them back to Europe on his second voyage. From there, Portuguese and Spanish explorers carried them around the world, spicing up the cuisines of Europe, Africa, India, and Asia. So Columbus is, at least, a culinary hero to me.

One of the first celebrations of Columbus was in 1792, when a ceremony organized by the Columbian Order was held in New York City honoring him and the 300th anniversary of his landing in the Bahamas. On October 12, 1866, the Italian population of New York organized the first celebration of the discovery of America. Three years later, Italians in San Francisco celebrated October 12, calling it C-Day.

To mark the 400th anniversary of Columbus's voyage, in 1892 President Benjamin Harrison made a proclamation. But it was Colorado that became the first state to observe a Columbus Day, in 1905. In 1937, President Franklin Roosevelt proclaimed every October 12 as Columbus Day. That's where it stayed until 1971, when the three-day-weekend legislators declared it a federal public holiday on the second Monday in October. To celebrate Barbecue Columbus Day, I've created a menu based on traditional Italian recipes.

Bread Salad with Grill-Roasted Tomatoes

Grilled Vegetable Soup

Smoked Italian Sausage Pizza on the Grill

Grill-Baked Rosemary and Garlic Potatoes

Grilled Escarole Salad

Polenta Cookies

▼▼▼▼

Bread Salad with Grill-Roasted Tomatoes

4 stale Italian or French rolls, split

4 tomatoes, sliced

2 tablespoons chopped Italian parsley

2 tablespoons balsamic vinegar

¼ cup extra virgin olive oil

Salt and freshly ground black pepper to taste

People have a tendency to forget about bread salad, but it's so tasty that I'm on a mission to revive it. This is a very simple Italian version. • **Yield: 4 servings**

Prepare the grill for direct cooking at high heat.

In a bowl, soak the bread in water for about 10 minutes, then drain and squeeze the bread to remove the excess water. Tear the bread into pieces and place in another bowl.

Grill the tomato slices for about 30 seconds per side, then remove and place in the bowl with the bread. Add the parsley, vinegar, olive oil, and salt and pepper and mix well.

Grilled Vegetable Soup

3 whole carrots, peeled

3 ribs celery

4 red bell peppers, sliced into long, thin strips

3 large onions, sliced thick

Two 14-ounce cans plum tomatoes, chopped

4 cups water

1 tablespoon minced fresh rosemary

1 teaspoon minced fresh oregano

Freshly grated Parmesan cheese

Grilling the vegetables caramelizes the sugar in them, making them sweeter than raw vegetables. Note that I'm using canned tomatoes, which is perfectly acceptable. Often, tomatoes that are canned when ripe taste better than fresh supermarket tomatoes. • **Yield: 6 servings**

Prepare the grill for direct cooking at high heat.

Grill the carrots, celery, peppers, and onions until they are browned and soft. Remove from the grill and dice them. Transfer the vegetables to a pot, add the tomatoes, cover, and simmer for 30 minutes.

Add the water, rosemary, and oregano and simmer uncovered for 15 minutes.

Transfer the soup to serving bowls and sprinkle the cheese over the top.

Smoked Italian Sausage Pizza on the Grill

2 Italian sausages

3 cups chopped fresh tomatoes, such as cherry or Roma

2 teaspoons crushed red chile

2 tablespoons chopped capers

2 tablespoons chopped black olives

1 tablespoon chopped fresh basil

One 12-inch prebaked pizza shell

Extra virgin olive oil

Garlic salt

1 cup freshly grated Pecorino Romano cheese

Italian sausage is one of my favorite links and I use it in spaghetti sauces and on pizzas such as this one. Pizza on the grill is something you really should try. I love it. Just make sure that the grate is very clean before you begin. Feel free to change the cheese as you like. • **Yield: 4 to 6 servings**

Prepare the grill for indirect cooking at 350°F, using apple wood for flavor.

Place the sausages on the grill and smoke them for 1 hour. Remove to a cutting board and remove the casing. Chop the sausages coarsely.

In a bowl, combine the sausage with the tomatoes, chile, capers, olives, and basil, and mix well.

Brush the pizza shell with olive oil. Place the pizza shell on the grate, spread the sausage mixture over it, sprinkle some garlic salt on top, and spread the cheese over the top. Close the cover of the grill and cook, rotating the pizza 90 degrees twice so it will cook evenly, until the crust is browned and the cheese is melted. This should take 5 to 10 minutes.

Grill-Baked Rosemary and Garlic Potatoes

4 large russet potatoes, peeled and diced

2 tablespoons minced fresh rosemary

2 tablespoons minced garlic

½ cup extra virgin olive oil

1 teaspoon salt

Freshly ground black pepper to taste

These tidbits make a great snack as well as a side dish. The trick to cooking them outdoors is to make sure that your grill cooks very hot, at least 400°F.

• Yield: 4 servings

Prepare the grill for indirect cooking at 400°F.

In a bowl, combine all ingredients and mix thoroughly. Spread the mixture in a single layer in a large, shallow roasting pan.

Place the pan on the grate, close the grill, and cook for about 1 hour, turning the potatoes every 15 minutes with a spatula. They should be crisp and brown when done.

Grilled Escarole Salad

2 heads of escarole

½ cup extra virgin olive oil

⅓ cup good-quality balsamic vinegar

Salt and freshly ground pepper to taste

This is a nice side dish that has a slightly smoky taste from being tossed right on the grill. Give it a try. I think you'll like it. • **Yield: 6 to 8 servings**

Clean the escarole well in several rinses of cold water and spin-dry in a salad spinner.

Toss with ¼ cup of the olive oil.

Heat the grill for direct cooking at high heat.

Toss the escarole directly onto the grate and toss as you would any salad, making sure no leaves get through the grate.

When the salad is wilted and just slightly charred, remove the escarole to a salad bowl. Add the remaining olive oil and the vinegar and toss to coat. Add salt and pepper as desired and serve at room temperature.

Polenta Cookies

1 cup seedless white raisins (sultanas)

2¼ cups milk

1 cup sugar

½ teaspoon salt

2½ cups cornmeal

1 cup all-purpose flour

½ cup butter

5 eggs

1¼ cups pine nuts

Freshly grated zest of 1 lemon

A few drops of vanilla extract

2 teaspoons baking powder

Confectioner's sugar

Here is an interesting twist on cookies that replaces most of the flour with cornmeal.

- **Yield: About 3 dozen cookies**

Preheat the oven to 400°F.

In a bowl, combine the raisins with warm water and let them soak for 10 minutes to soften them. Drain.

Heat the milk in a saucepan until boiling and add the sugar and salt. Slowly add the cornmeal and flour, stirring constantly. Reduce the heat and simmer for about 30 minutes, or until it is thick and creamy.

Pour the batter into a bowl and slowly add the butter. Add the eggs, 1 at time, constantly stirring so that the warm batter doesn't cook them. Once the eggs have been incorporated, add the raisins, pine nuts, zest, vanilla, and baking powder and mix well.

Grease a cookie sheet and drop tablespoonfuls of batter on it. Bake for about 25 minutes or until golden brown.

Eggtoberfest:
A Great Barbecue Event

▼▼

It's no secret that I am a big fan of the Big Green Egg. Just in case you don't know, it's a space-age ceramic grill/smoker that comes from Atlanta. It does a remarkable job of slow cooking for competition, and it's also the best direct grill I've ever used. Not to mention the alternate setups available for cooking pizza, bread, pies, and cakes. The Big Green Egg enthusiasts are so into it that we are lovingly referred to as a cult. This cult lives daily on the forum at www.biggreenegg.com, but every October there is a call to all eggers to return to the mother ship for a party, and party we do. The company puts on a meet-and-greet on Friday night, complete with many drinks and appetizers. But that's just a warm-up. Early Saturday morning the Eggs roll out. There is in excess of 100 new Eggs for any and all to cook on. The rules are simple. You pay your nominal fee at the door; then you cook, eat, and drink until you don't want to do those things anymore. It's a heck of a party. There is usually another impromptu cooking and drinking session in the parking lot of the hotel. This is known as the after party. This is no lightweight event, either. There are many regulars who cook and party and there is much interest in sharing recipes afterward, so Atlanta egger Bill Wise (Wise One) regularly assembles an Eggtoberfest virtual cookbook that he shares with all the eggers. So when I decided to feature Eggtoberfest in this book, I contacted Bill and he generously shared some legendary Eggtoberfest recipes. I thank him, and all those whose recipes are here.

Wise One's Bacon-Wrapped Scallops

YB's Bacon-Wrapped Watermelon Rinds

Grillmeister's ABTs on the Half Shell (Lovingly Known on the Internet as Atomic Buffalo Turds

Mad Max's Rolled Flank Steak

Tomato Pie from the Loves

J. Slot's Peach Cobbler

▼▼▼▼▼

Wise One's Bacon-Wrapped Scallops

1 pound lean bacon, thinly cut

1 pound sea scallops (should be about 24)

24 round toothpicks, soaked in water for at least 30 minutes

Favorite rub

½ cup lemon juice

½ cup maple syrup

Bill Wise can cook, too.

• **Yield: 4 to 6 servings as an appetizer**

About 4 hours before you plan to cook, take a piece of bacon and wrap it around each scallop. It may wrap twice but that's okay. Secure the bacon with a toothpick.

Sprinkle the exposed ends of the scallops with the rub. Place all the scallops in a container so that they are touching. Mix the lemon juice and maple syrup and pour over the scallops. Cover and place in the refrigerator for 3 to 4 hours.

Prepare the cooker for indirect cooking at 375°F.

Place the scallops on a seafood grill (or use a sheet of aluminum foil with holes punched into it over a regular grill) over a drip pan. Cook for 30 minutes.

YB's Bacon-Wrapped Watermelon Rinds

1 jar (16 ounces) pickled watermelon rind

1 pound bacon

24 round toothpicks, soaked in water for at least 30 minutes

What a combo! I'm glad Larry Ward, aka YB, thought of it, because I never would have.

- **Yield: Serves many as an appetizer**

Prepare the grill for indirect cooking at 350°F.

Wrap each pickled watermelon rind with a bacon slice and secure with a toothpick. Cook on a fish/veggie grid on a raised grill until the bacon is done. You have to watch them closely and rotate them often because with the high sugar content they burn easily.

Grillmeister's ABTs on the Half Shell (Lovingly Known on the Internet as Atomic Buffalo Turds)

30 fresh jalapeños, 2 to 3 inches long

Two 8-ounce packages cream cheese

1 pound bacon (may be more than you need)

60 Hillshire Farms Smokie Links

1 jar pre-minced garlic (fresh works great, too)

1 bottle Dizzy Pig Jamaican Firewalk rub (www.dizzypigbbq.com)

60 round toothpicks, soaked in water for at least 30 minutes

Ed Krach, aka Grillmeister, hosts Texas Eggfest, one of the many successful spinoffs of Eggtoberfest.

• Yield: Serves many as an appetizer

Wash and remove the stems of the jalapeños and halve them lengthwise. Remove seeds and veins, or leave veins in if you would like a hotter ABT.

Cut lengths of bacon strips just long enough to cover the jalapeños and fill the halves with cream cheese. Sprinkle the cheese liberally with the rub and press a Smokie Link onto the cheese. Top it off with a piece of bacon and use a round toothpick to hold it all together.

Prepare the cooker for direct cooking at 325° to 350°F and toss on a couple handfuls of soaked hickory chips. Smoke direct for 30 to 45 minutes on a raised grid. A smoker basket or pizza screen will help in putting a whole batch on the Egg at one time. No turning is necessary, but you do want to look for hot spots. When done, let sit for a few minutes.

To remove, press down on the toothpick first before picking the ATB up. That will make sure you get all the parts. It's best to use your right hand to pick one up to eat while your left hand holds a cold beer.

Mad Max's Rolled Flank Steak

**1 flank steak, at least
2 pounds, butterflied**

½ cup olive oil

¼ cup balsamic vinegar

**1 teaspoon herbes de
Provence**

**⅓ pound thinly sliced
prosciutto**

**3 yellow or orange
peppers, roasted on the
grill and peeled, seeds and
stems removed**

Dried basil as needed

**Freshly grated Parmesan
cheese as needed**

Egg cooking runs in the Mad Max family. His lovely
daughter, Sydney, makes a mean meat loaf.

- **Yield: About 4 servings**

Note: This recipe needs advance preparation.

You can ask your butcher to butterfly the flank steak or you can do it yourself. Lay the steak flat, using a long knife to slice it into 2 thin halves by keeping the knife parallel to the cutting board. Depending on your pan/dish, you can leave it in 1 big flat piece or slice completely through it and have 2 pieces, which are easier to work into 2 small rolls. It's easier to slice through if you put the steak flat in the freezer for about 30 minutes so that it is a little stiff.

The night before you plan to cook, whisk together the oil, vinegar, and herbs. Put the steak in a zip bag and pour the mixture over it. Refrigerate.

Prepare the grill for indirect cooking at at 375°F.

Lay out the marinated butterflied flank steak, reserving the marinade, cover it evenly with a layer of the prosciutto, and spread the roasted peppers along one long edge (they should cover about one-fourth to one-third of the steak).

Sprinkle liberally with the basil and Parmesan cheese and roll tightly into 1 or 2 logs. (You may need to use some toothpicks to hold them together.)

Lay them in a pan that can go on the grill. Drizzle some of the leftover marinade on them. Cook for about 45 minutes for medium doneness. Remove to a platter, tent loosely with foil, and let rest for 10 minutes.

Slice thinly across the grain.

Tomato Pie from the Loves

3 or 4 ripe tomatoes
(heirloom are our
favorites)

Salt

One 9-inch deep-dish pie
crust

1 cup grated mozzarella
cheese

1 cup grated sharp white
cheddar cheese

1 cup mayonnaise (we
used Miracle Whip for the
Eggtoberfest)

8 fresh basil leaves, sliced
thinly

½ cup chopped green
onions

The Loves make one of my favorite dishes from any Eggtoberfest. • **Yield: 8 servings**

Prepare the cooker for indirect cooking at 350°F.

Peel and slice the tomatoes, put them into a colander, and sprinkle them with salt. Let drain 10 minutes.

While they're draining, bake the pie crust on the Egg at 350°F for about 10 minutes.

Mix the two cheeses and the mayonnaise or Miracle Whip together in a bowl and set aside.

Once the pie crust is done, remove it from the Egg and let it cool a few minutes. Raise the temp of the Egg to 400°F.

Layer the tomatoes, basil, and green onions and repeat till the pie crust is full. Spread the cheese mixture on top evenly.

Bake the pie until the top is browned lightly, about 45 minutes. Remove from the Egg and let stand for 10 minutes. Slice and serve.

J. Slot's Peach Cobbler

1 can (29 ounces) peaches, drained

1 cup sugar

¾ stick butter

1 cup self-rising flour

½ cup milk

Jim Slotterback has a competition team called the Big Green Eggomaniacs. I think he's into it.

• **Yield: About 6 servings**

Prepare the cooker for indirect cooking at 350°F. Place the drained peaches in a bowl, sprinkle liberally with some sugar, and set aside for about 15 to 20 minutes.

Meanwhile, melt the butter and pour it into the pan you will cook the cobbler in.

In another bowl, mix the flour, remaining sugar, and milk together to form a batter.

Place the peaches in the pan with the melted butter. Pour the batter over the top of the peaches, going back and forth (as if you were painting the top) until all the batter is used.

Cook the cobbler until the top is nicely browned. (The time varies on this one, so you'll have to watch it closely.)

Halloween:
Pumpkin Grill and More

▼▼▼

Halloween is the best holiday of the year for people who like to cross-dress and beg. I must admit that while I've participated in many counterculture activities, cross-dressing has never made the list, even on Halloween. It might be because there just aren't any good dresses in my size. Most people have no idea what Halloween really means and why it's called that. Well, here you go. When Christianity became the primary religion in Europe, November 1 became All Saints' Day—a day to honor the saints who, for some unknown reason, didn't have a day dedicated solely to them, as Patrick does in Part 2 of this book. The mass performed on All Saints' Day became known as "Allhallowmass" ("hallow" meaning to make holy), and the night before became known as All Hallow's Evening, condensed to All Hallow's E'en, and

further reduced to Hallowe'en or Halloween. See how easy that was? Now the tough question: Why dress up in costume?

To answer a question with a question: Trick or treat?

The tradition of going door to door and begging for candy on Halloween seems to go back to the Druids, and why it originated is not clear. But if you went begging, you were bound to get turned down, so the saying "trick or treat" was born, and that created a problem: If you pulled a trick, people would know who you were. But not if you were in costume. I might point out here that some barbecue aprons, hats, and gloves closely resemble a costume, so if you've got them, all you need to dress up for the Halloween Barbecue Feast that follows is a mask like the Lone Ranger's. Shave your mustache, too.

Allspiced Cider

**Smoked Sausage, Leek, and Potato Soup
Served in a Pumpkin**

Short Ribs with Baby Bellas and Port Wine

Homemade Noodles

Pumpkin Cheesecake

▼▼▼▼▼

Allspiced Cider

1 tablespoon whole allspice

One 3-inch cinnamon stick

3 cups apple cider

1 cup orange juice

½ lemon, sliced

1 teaspoon honey

¼ cup brandy

There's nothing like a spiced cider to get you ready to beg for candy. If you can find hard cider, you can eliminate the brandy here. Serve with a cinnamon stick in each cup if you want. • **Yield: 6 servings**

Tie the allspice in a piece of cheesecloth. Place in a medium saucepan along with the cinnamon stick, cider, orange juice, lemon slices, and honey. Bring to a boil. Reduce the heat and simmer, covered, for 5 minutes.

Remove the spice bag and stir in the brandy.

Smoked Sausage, Leek, and Potato Soup Served in a Pumpkin

4 tablespoons butter

2 tablespoons olive oil

2 cups leeks, washed well, halved, and sliced

3 cups peeled and cubed russet potatoes

2 cups cubed smoked sausage*

2 cloves garlic

1 quart water

2 vegetable bouillon cubes (I prefer Knorr brand)

1 tablespoon coarsely ground black pepper

1 teaspoon dried oregano

1 teaspoon dried tarragon

½ teaspoon ground nutmeg

1 medium pie pumpkin, top and stem removed and reserved, inside cleaned

*You can use store-bought sausage, but I like to use a 1-pound roll of breakfast sausage that is smoked at 225°F until it reaches an internal temp of 170°F.

I think this is my favorite recipe from this book. It's a delicious hearty soup that's served in a pumpkin. The kids will love it. Be sure to wear heavy gloves when carrying the pumpkin into the dining room or you'll have quite a mess. • **Yield: 6 servings**

Prepare the cooker for indirect cooking at 275°F.

In a Dutch oven over medium heat, melt the butter with the oil. Add the leeks and cook for 2 minutes. Add the potatoes and cook for about 5 minutes, stirring occasionally. Add the sausage and garlic and cook about another 5 minutes, or until everything is getting soft. Add the water, bouillon, pepper, oregano, tarragon, and nutmeg and bring to a boil. Reduce to a simmer and cook for 20 minutes.

Place the cleaned pumpkin on a deep-dish pizza pan that you'll always use for cooking on the grill or smoker. Pour the soup into the pumpkin. Replace the top on the pumpkin and place it in the cooker.

Cook for about 1 hour, but watch it so the pumpkin doesn't get too soft and collapse.

When the pumpkin feels tender, carefully take it off the cooker and bring it inside. Stir and then serve. I like to scrape some of the pumpkin away from the sides to serve with the soup.

Short Ribs with Baby Bellas and Port Wine

3 to 4 pounds beef short ribs

Dr. BBQ's Five Spice Salt (page 282)

1 pound baby portobello mushrooms, sliced

3 cloves garlic, crushed

¾ cup port wine

¾ cup beef broth

• Yield: 4 to 6 servings

Prepare the cooker for indirect cooking at 250°F, using cherry wood for flavor.

Season the ribs liberally with the Five Spice Salt and put them in the cooker. Cook until they are nicely browned, about 2 hours.

Put the ribs in an aluminum foil pan. Spread the baby bellas and the garlic on the ribs evenly. Pour the wine and beef broth over the top. Cover with foil and return to the cooker. Raise the temp to 350°F and cook until the ribs are tender. This should take about another 2 hours. Check occasionally to make sure the liquid hasn't dried up, and add some more broth and wine as needed.

Remove the ribs to a platter, spoon the bellas into a bowl, and add as much of the liquid as you desire. Serve with the homemade noodles on the following page.

Homemade Noodles

3 cups semolina flour (available in gourmet shops and health food stores)

2 large eggs, beaten lightly

1 tablespoon olive oil

I thought that these noodles would go well with the short ribs. If you are making them a day ahead, store them in the refrigerator. • **Yield: About ½ to ¾ pound noodles**

Place the flour in a mixing board. Make a well in the middle and place the eggs and olive oil in it.

Mix with your hands and then knead for 10 minutes. Cover the dough and let it sit for 30 minutes.

Using a rolling pin (or a pasta machine), roll the dough very thin (1⁄32 inch or less). Cut it into 1½-inch-wide strips.

Cook the noodles in boiling salted water for 1 to 2 minutes—no more. Drain, place on a kitchen towel, and cover with plastic wrap until you are ready to use them in your recipe or serve them.

Pumpkin Cheesecake

The Crust

1 cup graham cracker crumbs

3 tablespoons butter or margarine, melted

2 tablespoons sugar

The Filling

2 packages (8 ounces each) cream cheese, softened

1¼ cups sugar

1 can (16 ounces) solid-pack pumpkin (not pumpkin-pie mix)

¾ cup sour cream

2 tablespoons whiskey or 2 teaspoons vanilla extract

1 teaspoon ground cinnamon

½ teaspoon ground allspice

¼ teaspoon salt

4 large eggs

The Topping

1 cup sour cream

3 tablespoons sugar

1 teaspoon vanilla extract

Tired of pumpkin pie? Then try this fancy pumpkin cheesecake. Sip a little of that leftover whiskey to aid your digestion. . . . . • **Yield: 16 servings**

Preheat the oven to 350°F.

In a 9 × 3-inch springform pan, using a fork, stir the graham cracker crumbs, melted butter or margarine, and sugar until moistened. With your hand, press the mixture onto the bottom of the pan. Tightly wrap the outside of the pan with heavy-duty foil to prevent leakage when baking in a water bath later. Bake the crust 10 minutes. Cool completely in the pan on a wire rack.

In a large bowl, with a mixer at medium speed, beat the cream cheese until smooth; slowly beat in the sugar until blended, about 1 minute, scraping the bowl often with a rubber spatula.

With the mixer at low speed, beat in the pumpkin, sour cream, whiskey or vanilla, cinnamon, allspice, and salt. Add the eggs, 1 at a time, beating just until blended after each addition. Pour the pumpkin mixture into the crust and place in a large roasting pan.

Place the pan on an oven rack. Carefully pour enough boiling water into the pan to come 1 inch up the sides of the springform pan. Bake the cheesecake for 1 hour 10 minutes, or until the center barely jiggles.

Meanwhile, prepare the sour-cream topping: In a small bowl, using a wire whisk, beat the sour cream, sugar, and vanilla until blended.

Remove the cheesecake from the water bath, leaving the water bath in the oven, and spread the sour-cream mixture evenly over the top. Return the cake to the water bath and bake 5 minutes longer. Remove the cheesecake to a wire rack and discard the foil. With a small knife, loosen the cheesecake from the sides of the pan to help prevent cracking during cooling. Cool the cheesecake completely.

Cover and refrigerate the cheesecake for at least 6 hours or overnight, until well chilled. Remove the side of pan to serve.

Melbourne Cup Day:
Barbecue in Australia

▼▼

Barbecue is growing in Australia as well as everywhere else, and I had to figure out a way to get some Australian-style barbecue in this book. So I looked up a holiday celebrated in Oz that would be sure to cause a mass firing up of the barbies. I found the biggest horse race Down Under, the Melbourne Cup. Held the first Tuesday in November, which is the Australian spring, Melbourne Cup Day is a public holiday over much of the country. The race is long, nearly two miles, and has a prize of more than $2 million, so it's a pretty big deal. Gambling and barbecue, what a great combination.

Of course, the race only lasts a few minutes, so what are you going to do with the rest of the day? Well, if you're at the race, you'll be drinking and showing off. "Fashions on the Field" is a major activity, with substantial prizes awarded for the best-dressed female and more recently, male racegoers. In 1965 a famous supermodel shocked everyone by showing up in a mini-skirt! Horrors.

If you're not at the race showing off your fashion sense, then you're probably sightseeing, going to the beach or mountains, having a picnic, or throwing a barbie party (no, not with dolls) like this one.

Grilled Mango Salad

Shrimp on the Barbie

Australian Dinkum Chili

Shortbread Biscuits

▼▼▼▼▼

Grilled Mango Salad

2 large ripe mangoes, peeled

1 large cucumber, peeled and sliced into strips

3 teaspoons freshly squeezed lime juice

1 tablespoon sugar

2 teaspoons freshly grated ginger, or more to taste

Here is a great tropical salad that goes well with grilled seafood. You can add a sliced banana if you want. • **Yield: 4 servings**

Prepare the grill for direct cooking at high heat.

Slice the "cheeks" from the mangoes and place them on the grill. Grill for about 90 seconds a side, remove to a cutting board, and cut into strips. Place the mango and cucumber strips in a bowl.

In another bowl, combine the remaining ingredients and mix well. Pour this over the mango and cucumber slices and serve.

Shrimp on the Barbie

1 stick butter, melted

¼ cup olive oil

1 tablespoon dried oregano

1 tablespoon dried marjoram

2 tablespoons minced fresh Italian parsley

3 tablespoons freshly squeezed lemon juice

3 cloves garlic, minced

1 tablespoon minced shallot

Salt and freshly ground black pepper to taste

1½ pounds large shrimp, unpeeled

Spinach leaves

Lemon slices

If you search Google for the phrase "shrimp on the barbie," you will get more than 16,000 results, which is an indication of how many variations there are on this theme. Here is my favorite, which is really easy to make.

• **Yield: 6 servings**

Prepare the grill for direct cooking at medium-high heat.

Combine the butter, olive oil, herbs, lemon juice, garlic, shallot, and salt and pepper in a bowl. Add the shrimp and marinate at room temperature for 1 hour or in the refrigerator for 5 hours, stirring occasionally.

Thread the shrimp on small metal skewers. Grill the shrimp for about 2 minutes per side.

Line a platter with spinach leaves and arrange the skewers on top. Add lemon slices for garnish.

Australian Dinkum Chili

½ pound bacon

2 tablespoons vegetable oil

2 onions, coarsely chopped

1 celery stalk, coarsely chopped

1 green bell pepper, chopped

2 pounds top sirloin, cut into 1-inch cubes

1 pound beef, coarsely ground

1 pound smoked pork, chopped fine

4 tablespoons hot red chile powder

3 tablespoons mild red chile powder

2 cloves garlic, minced

1 tablespoon dried oregano

1 teaspoon ground cumin

1 large can Foster's beer

One 14.5-ounce can whole tomatoes

1 boomerang (optional but authentic; available at sporting goods stores)

3 teaspoons brown sugar

"Fair dinkum" is an Australian expression meaning authentic. So I guess if some Aussie stole this chili fair and square from Texas and added some Down Under touches, it's authentic as can be. • **Yield: 8 to 10 servings**

Fry the bacon in a skillet over medium heat. Drain the strips on paper towels. Chop into ½-inch pieces and reserve.

Heat the oil in a large, heavy pot over medium heat. Add the onions, celery, and bell pepper and cook until the onions are translucent, about 5 minutes.

Combine all the beef and pork with the chile powders, garlic, oregano, and cumin. Add this meat-and-spice mixture to the pot. Break up any lumps with a fork and cook, stirring occasionally, until the meat is evenly browned.

Add the beer, tomatoes, and reserved bacon to the pot. Bring to a boil, then lower the heat and simmer, uncovered, for 1½ hours.

Wave the boomerang over the pot 7 times each 30 minutes from this point on. Taste, adjust the seasonings, and add more beer, if desired. Simmer for 2½ hours longer.

Add the brown sugar and simmer for 15 minutes longer, vigorously waving the boomerang over the pot.

Shortbread Biscuits

2 sticks butter

1 cup confectioner's sugar

1½ cups sifted all-purpose flour

1 cup cornstarch

Pinch of salt

These so-called biscuits are really cookies, and they make a fine finale to Melbourne Cup Day.

• **Yield: About 25 biscuits**

Preheat the oven to 350°F.

In a bowl, cream the butter and sugar until light and fluffy. Add the sifted flour, cornstarch, and salt and mix well. Turn out onto a lightly floured board and knead lightly.

Divide the dough in half, and shape into 2 rolls 1½ inches wide and 6 inches long. Wrap in plastic wrap, and refrigerate for 1 hour or until firm.

Cut the rolls into ¼-inch slices and place on baking sheets. Bake for 15 minutes.

Football Tailgating:
Yet More Portable Grilling

▼▼

According to the Commissioner of Tailgating, aka Joe Cahn, "Tailgating dates back to the very first college football game between Rutgers and Princeton in 1869, when fans traveled to the game by carriage, grilling sausages and burgers at the 'tail end' of the horse." I think the commissioner might have made that one up. I met Joe once and asked him what he did at tailgate parties. "I'm the commissioner," he replied. I told him I understood that and I wasn't being disrespectful of his title, but what exactly was his role when he attended a party and simply said, "I'm the commissioner"? My thought was that I had found a guy with a better job than me.

Wherever tailgating began, it sure has been a good idea. A whole industry has sprung up because of it, complete with specialized grills that hang on the back of your vehicle, handbooks, games, videos, chairs, trailers, and tables. Of course these things all become more valuable when produced in your team's colors.

There are legendary tailgating parties all around the country, but the largest one anywhere happens in my state, Florida, during the Georgia-Florida football game in Jacksonville. It's called the World's Largest Cocktail Party, and fans start arriving Wednesday for the Saturday game. Many are still partying on Sunday afternoon. Where they sleep is unknown. Maybe they don't. I think the Florida fans should be called "tailgators."

My tailgate menus always include a cooler of beer, an interesting alternate drink, and, of course, soda and water for the designated drivers. I always bring the grill, but I also like to bring a few made-ahead things so the party can get started right away. I also like to make the dessert, something like cookies or brownies that are available the whole time. I'm always amazed at how many people want their dessert first.

The Michelada

Swimming Smoked Salmon

Cookshack Salmon Brine

Red Chile–Marinated Rib-Eye Steak Sandwiches

Tailgating Spaghetti Salad

Daiquiri Tarts

▼▼▼▼

The Michelada

¼ cup soy sauce

¼ cup freshly squeezed lime juice (key lime preferred)

¼ cup Worcestershire sauce

1 teaspoon hot sauce of choice, or more to taste

½ teaspoon freshly ground black pepper

Tailgate partyers are experimenting with the latest enhancement to a cold beer: the *michelada*. The word roughly translates as "my cold brewski." I first learned of this new drink from Dave DeWitt's Web site www.fieryfoods.com, and it seemed like a great addition to a tailgate party. Just make a jug of the mix and offer it up to your guests as an accompaniment to their beers.

• Yield: 1 drink

Combine all the ingredients in a jar and shake well. To serve, place 1 jigger of the mix in a tall glass. Fill the glass with ice and pour in the beer of choice.

Swimming Smoked Salmon

A Recipe from Barbecue All Star Stuart Powell

Smoked salmon is a great starter for a tailgate party. You can put it out right away with some drinks, and the crowd will leave you alone while you get the grill going. This version is for a whole salmon, and it makes for a great presentation. I don't usually much care for salmon but it was on the buffet at Stuart's house recently, and the presentation was pretty neat so I tried some. It was really good, so I asked Stuart to be one of the Barbecue All Stars in this book. It's no stretch for Stuart to step in as such as he is the CEO and driving force behind Cookshack, the smoker company from Ponca City, Oklahoma. Cookshack has been making smokers since the '60s and continues to grow. That should be no surprise, as they build great little smokers for home use, great big smokers for commercial use, and all sizes in between. If you look in my backyard you'll see one. Stuart is also a first-class barbecue cook. I often see him at shows doing the cooking for his team.

- **Yield: 6 to 8 servings, or more as part of a buffet**

Note: This recipe requires a whole bunch of advance preparation, but it is worth the trouble. You'll need to start about 36 hours before you plan to eat.

One 5- to 6-pound cleaned whole salmon, including the head and tail

Cookshack Salmon Brine (recipe follows)

Lemon slices for garnish

1 jar capers, drained, for garnish

1 jar pickled pearl onions, drained, for garnish

Place the salmon in the brine and refrigerate. Allow the salmon to brine a minimum of 12 hours and maximum of 24. Remove from the brine, rinse with cold water, pat dry, and refrigerate, uncovered, for 6 hours.

Prepare the cooker for indirect cooking at 180°F, using cherry wood for flavor.

Stand the salmon up with the cavity spread and the flesh of the fish facing the heat. You'll need to make a triangular frame out of aluminum foil and put it underneath the fish to help it stand up. Cook for 4 hours.

Remove to a baking sheet, tent with foil, and let cool for 1 hour. Transfer to the refrigerator and cool for at least 4 hours.

Remove from the refrigerator and make a cut in the skin down the back. Then make a cut down in front of the tail and behind the gills. Peel the skin away from the sides.

To serve, stand the salmon up on a plate that's garnished with lemon slices, capers, and pickled pearl onions. This re-creates the bottom of a river where a salmon would rest.

Serve with crackers.

Cookshack Salmon Brine

1 gallon water

1 cup kosher salt

1 cup brown sugar

1 cup lemon juice

1 tablespoon minced garlic

1 tablespoon freshly
ground black pepper

1 teaspoon Morton's
Tenderquick

• **Yield: About 1 gallon**

Note: This must be made ahead of time and chilled.

Mix 1 quart of the water with all the remaining ingredients in a large pot. Heat on the stove until the brine solution is hot; however, do not bring it to a boil.

Remove the brine from the stove and add the remaining cold water. Allow the brine to cool. Check the brine to ensure that it will float a whole raw egg. If the egg does not float, add kosher salt to the brine until the egg will float. Chill before using.

Red Chile–Marinated Rib-Eye Steak Sandwiches

½ cup hot red chile powder

¼ cup olive oil

3 cloves garlic, minced

Salt and freshly ground black pepper to taste

2 large rib-eye steaks

4 large rolls

Mayonnaise

4 leaves romaine lettuce

8 thin tomato slices

Here's the ideal tailgating sandwich, flavored with the tasty and spicy red chile powder from New Mexico.

• **Yield: 4 servings**

Note: This recipe requires advance preparation.

In a bowl, combine the chile powder, olive oil, garlic, and salt and pepper and mix well. Rub this paste over the steaks and let them marinate, covered, for at least 2 hours, but preferably overnight.

Prepare the grill for direct cooking at high heat. Grill the steaks for about 12 to 15 minutes, turning often. Cut into one to check that it's medium rare.

Open the rolls and spread mayonnaise over each. Cut the steaks in half and place each half on the roll. Top with the lettuce and tomato slices.

Tailgating Spaghetti Salad

1 pound mozzarella cheese

5 ripe tomatoes, peeled, seeded, and coarsely chopped

1 cup coarsely chopped fresh basil leaves

2 cloves garlic, minced

2 tablespoons salt

3 tablespoons olive oil

1 pound thin spaghetti

Salt and freshly ground black pepper to taste

This side dish is designed to be served in the parking lot along with the steak sandwiches.

• **Yield: At least 8 servings as a side dish**

Bring a large pot of water to a boil.

Cut the mozzarella into small cubes and set aside in a small bowl. Combine the tomatoes, basil, and garlic in another bowl.

When the water is boiling hard, add the salt and olive oil. Add the spaghetti and cook just until it is al dente. Do not overcook. Quickly drain the spaghetti and return it at once to the warm pot.

Immediately stir in the mozzarella; the heat of the pasta will melt it slightly. Stir in the contents of the other bowl. Season to taste with salt and pepper. Transfer to a serving bowl and reserve until needed. If holding more than a couple of hours, refrigerate, but serve at room temperature.

Daiquiri Tarts

½ cup freshly squeezed lime juice

1 tablespoon light rum

½ cup sugar

2 large eggs, slightly beaten

1 strip lime zest, 1 by 2 inches

1 package frozen 3-inch pastry shells (not puff pastry)

2 tablespoons melted unsalted butter

2 tablespoons confectioner's sugar

½ cup whipped cream

Made with the ingredients of the famous drink, these tangy tarts are quick and delicious. If you can find them, use the key or Mexican limes instead of the larger Persian limes. • **Yield: 12 tarts**

Note: Prepare these ahead to top off the tailgating.

In the top of a double boiler, combine the lime juice, rum, sugar, eggs, and zest. Set the top over (not in) lightly boiling water and whisk the mixture constantly until thick enough to coat the back of a spoon, about 5 minutes. Strain the mixture into a bowl and allow to cool to room temperature, whisking occasionally.

Heat the oven to 400°F. Arrange the pastry shells on a baking sheet and bake until firm and lightly browned. Brush the shells with the melted butter and sprinkle the confectioners' sugar over them. Return the shells to the oven and bake for 3 to 5 minutes or until golden brown.

Divide the lime mixture among the shells and top with a dollop of whipped cream.

Willis Carrier's Birthday:
A Barbecue Salute to the Father of Cool

▼▼

The inventor of real, working air-conditioning was born on November 26, 1876. Carrier's first big invention was a dehumidifier that shortened the time it took to dry macaroni. "We ruined a lot of macaroni," reported one of his associates. In 1915 Willis and six other engineers formed the Carrier Engineering Corporation with a starting capital of $35,000. In 1995 sales topped $5 billion. Why didn't my grandfather invest in some of that action? The first buildings to use air conditioners were fancy hotels and the theaters. There is a raging debate among air conditioner aficionados as to which theaters were first cooled down. Some say it was three theaters in Texas and others claim it was the famous Grauman's Metropolitan in Los Angeles. By 1929 Congress was generating so much hot air that Carrier was called in to cool down the United States Capitol. Air-conditioning was a luxury until after World War II, when it became standard in construction.

Technically, "The Father of Cool" did not invent the very first system to cool a building, but his system was the first successful and safe device that started the science of modern air-conditioning. I'm really glad he did that, so we're gonna barbecue to celebrate his birthday.

Tuna Kabobs

Smoked Cornish Hens

Old Hen Brine

Linguine with Cilantro and Parsley Pesto

Flourless Chocolate Torte

▼▼▼▼▼

Tuna Kabobs

1½ pounds fresh tuna steak, cut into 1 ½-inch cubes

Dr. BBQ's Soy Sauce Marinade (page 293)

6 to 8 bamboo skewers, soaked in water for at least 1 hour

I recently heard tuna called "the other red meat." I think that is a great description. • **Yield: About 6 servings**

About 4 hours before you plan to cook, put the tuna in a zip bag. Pour the marinade over it and refrigerate.

Prepare the grill for direct cooking at high heat.

Thread the tuna evenly on the skewers. Place them directly on the grill. Cook for 30 seconds on each of the 4 sides. That's it. The tuna is to be eaten very rare.

Smoked Cornish Hens

6 Cornish hens

Old Hen Brine (recipe follows)

Dr. BBQ's Chicken Seasoning (page 281)

When I cook Cornish hens, they make me feel like somebody's grandma. If those hens would just eat a little more as they grow up they could be big and strong like their big brother, the chicken. But of course they aren't supposed to be any bigger than the 16 to 24 ounces that they are. But I still feel that they need some help plumping up during cooking, so I like to brine them. I'm not a big fan of salty brines, and I'm not really trying to preserve them like the folks that invented brining, so I just back down on the salt. I'm sure some purists will say that this is actually a marinade instead of a brine. That's okay with me. It tastes good and makes the hens nice and juicy, so you can call it what you like. • **Yield: 6 or more servings**

Note: The hens stay in the brine for only 3 hours, but you'll have to make the brine the day before so it can get cooled down and then chilled in the refrigerator.

Place the hens in a large plastic or glass container and cover with the brine. Put them in the refrigerator for 3 hours. Remove the container from the refrigerator and pour off the brine. Fill the container with fresh water and pour off, to rinse the hens 3 separate times. Dry the hens with paper towels and return them to the refrigerator to dry.

Prepare the cooker for indirect cooking at 300°F, using apple wood for flavor.

When the cooker is ready, remove the hens from the refrigerator and season lightly with Dr. BBQ's Chicken Seasoning. Place the hens on the grate and cook about 1 hour, or until the internal temp of the thigh is 180°F and that of the breast is 160°F. These can be served whole as 1 per guest, or cut into halves or quarters and served with an additional main dish.

Old Hen Brine

1 gallon water

¾ cup kosher salt

1 cup brown sugar

1 tablespoon finely ground black pepper

1 tablespoon granulated garlic

1 tablespoon onion powder

1 tablespoon dried thyme

• Yield: A little more than 1 gallon

Note: This must be made ahead of time and chilled.

Place all the ingredients in a pot and bring to a simmer, stirring occasionally. Remove from the heat and cool.

Transfer to a plastic or glass container and refrigerate overnight.

Linguine with Cilantro and Parsley Pesto

1½ pounds linguine

½ cup chopped fresh basil

½ cup chopped fresh cilantro

2 cups chopped Italian parsley

1 cup chicken stock

¼ cup olive oil

4 tablespoons toasted pignoli nuts

4 tablespoons freshly grated Parmesan cheese

3 teaspoons crushed garlic

2 pasilla chiles, rehydrated, seeds and stems removed, chopped

When I cook up a recipe like this, I ask myself, "What beer goes best with pesto?" I think pilsner would be best. • **Yield: At least 12 servings as a side dish**

In a large pot, cook the pasta according to the directions on the package, until the pasta is al dente. Drain the pasta in a colander and place it in a serving bowl.

While the pasta is cooking, in a food processor blend the basil leaves, cilantro leaves, parsley, stock, olive oil, pignolis, cheese, garlic, and chiles. Pour over the pasta and toss well. Serve immediately.

Flourless Chocolate Torte

The Torte

2 cups unblanched almonds

Freshly grated zest of 3 oranges

3 ounces bittersweet chocolate, grated

1½ teaspoons ground cinnamon

6 eggs, separated and at room temperature

½ cup sugar

3 tablespoons freshly squeezed orange juice

3 tablespoons Grand Marnier

The Glaze

5 ounces bittersweet chocolate

1 tablespoon light corn syrup

¾ cup unsalted butter

Mexican Ibarra chocolate can replace the bittersweet chocolate and cinnamon in this torte. This dessert can be made up to a day in advance and should be kept at room temperature. • **Yield: 10 to 12 servings**

Preheat the oven to 350°F.

Butter the bottom and sides of a 9-inch springform pan, line it with parchment paper, and butter and flour the parchment paper.

Roast the almonds on a baking sheet for 5 minutes or until slightly browned. Cool. Place them in a blender or food processor and grind finely.

Combine the almonds, orange zest, grated chocolate, and cinnamon.

Beat the egg yolks until light, incorporating as much air as possible. When thick, add the sugar in 2 parts.

In another bowl, beat the egg whites until stiff. Beat the dry ingredients, orange juice, and one-third of the egg whites into the egg yolks, then rapidly fold in the remaining egg whites.

Pour the batter into the pan and bake in the middle of the oven for 35 to 40 minutes, or until the cake pulls away from the sides of the pan. Loosen the sides of the pan and cool for 10 minutes. Invert onto a rack to cool and remove the paper. When cool, paint with the Grand Marnier.

To make the glaze, break the chocolate into small pieces and combine all the ingredients in the top of a double boiler. Heat the pan and turn off as the water comes to a boil. Beat with a whisk until smooth.

Place the cake on a rack over a pan or waxed paper and pour half of the glaze in the center. Tilt the cake to distribute the glaze evenly and allow the cake to sit for 45 minutes. Repeat with remaining glaze and let sit for 45 minutes more before serving.

Thanksgiving:
The Ultimate Turkey and More

Most of what you think you know about Thanksgiving is just not true, but that doesn't make the holiday any less enjoyable. It is widely written that the first Thanksgiving occurred in 1621 and was celebrated by the Pilgrims, English settlers, and Indians, and that turkey was served. None of this is true. The first English Thanksgiving event occurred in 1578 in Newfoundland and, of course, Native Americans had celebrated the harvest for thousands of years before the English invasion. The 1621 event was probably a harvest celebration, but not a "day of thanksgiving," which implies fasting and prayer. The supposed Pilgrims (the settlers of Plymouth Colony) did not call themselves that but rather "Separatists" because they had left the Church of England. The term "Pilgrim" was invented much later by "historians" who wanted to make the event more romantic. There is no documentation that turkey was served, and more likely the feast included fish and corn. There are, however, mentions of wild turkeys in some of the colonists' writings. From 1777 to 1783, Thanksgiving Day, as declared by Congress, was celebrated in December. But in 1789 George Washington decreed that Thursday, November 26, was to be a day when "we may then all unite in rendering unto Him our sincere and humble thanks." Later presidents ordered that Thanksgiving be celebrated at various times, and in 1815, James Madison declared *two* Thanksgiving days. It wasn't until 1863 that Abraham Lincoln finally settled the situation by proclaiming the fourth Thursday in November to be a "National Day of Thanksgiving." It was not celebrated in the South because it was viewed as a Yankee event until the 1890s. Today, of course, Thanksgiving is a nonreligious holiday featuring parades, football, the beginning of the holiday season shopping, and turkey. Benjamin Franklin wrote: "I wish the Bald Eagle had not been chosen as the representative of our country: he is a Bird of bad moral character: like those among Men who live by Sharping and Robbing, he is generally poor and very often lousy. The Turkey is a much more respectable Bird and withal a true original Native of North America." I'll add that he tastes really good, too.

In my world, we are thankful for barbecue.

Hot Cranberry Drink

Orange Gold Salad

The Ultimate Turkey

Dr. BBQ's Pulled Pork Stuffing

Green Bean Smoked Casserole

Whiskey and Chocolate Pecan Pie

▼▼▼▼

Hot Cranberry Drink

2 cups fresh or frozen cranberries

6 cups water

1 cup sugar

¼ cup pepper jelly

7 whole cloves

½ cup freshly squeezed orange juice

¼ cup freshly squeezed lemon juice

Why serve cranberries in a jelly when you can just drink them? This is the perfect starter for the Thanksgiving dinner. I like to add a little vodka, too.

• Yield: 6 to 8 servings

In a saucepan, cook the cranberries in 2 cups of the water until they pop. Strain through a fine sieve, reserving the juice and discarding the skins; set aside.

In a large saucepan, combine the sugar, pepper jelly, cloves, and remaining water. Cook for 5 minutes over medium heat.

Add the orange and lemon juices and reserved cranberry juice and heat through. Remove the cloves. Serve hot.

Orange Gold Salad

1 cup coarsely grated carrot

2 oranges or 3 tangerines, peeled, sliced into thin rounds, seeds removed

¼ cup finely chopped shallots

½ teaspoon minced fresh basil

2 tablespoons grated fresh ginger

3 tablespoons rice vinegar

2 tablespoons olive oil

¼ teaspoon freshly ground white pepper

2 heads Boston lettuce, washed

Here is a nearly perfect Thanksgiving salad.
• Yield: 4 servings

In a medium glass bowl, toss together the carrot, orange rounds, and shallots. Then mix the basil, ginger, vinegar, oil, and pepper in a glass jar and shake thoroughly. Pour the dressing over the carrot mixture and toss gently. Chill for an hour or two before serving over the lettuce.

The Ultimate Turkey

One 12-pound turkey

Scottie's Creole Butter
(page 298)

Dr. BBQ's Creole Seasoning
(page 283)

Many people like to cook their turkey on those upright stands, so I thought I'd try it. I liked it so much I'm calling it The Ultimate Turkey. I use a pan underneath the whole thing so the juices can accumulate and steam underneath the turkey. You can reserve the juice then and use it in a gravy if you like.

• **Yield: About 12 servings**

Note: This recipe requires advance preparation.

The night before you plan to cook, inject the turkey all over with Scottie's Creole Butter. Wrap it in a big plastic bag and refrigerate overnight.

On Thanksgiving morning, before you tune into the Thanksgiving Day parades, prepare the cooker for indirect cooking at 325°F, using apple wood for flavor.

Season the turkey liberally with the Creole Seasoning. Place the turkey on the stand, and stand the whole thing up in a pan. If you have any reserved marinade, add it to the pan.

Place the turkey in the cooker and cook until the internal temp of the white meat is 160°F, and that of the dark meat is 180°F. This will take about 3 hours.

Remove the turkey to a platter. Tent it loosely and let it rest for 20 minutes. Carve and serve.

Dr. BBQ's Pulled Pork Stuffing

½ cup butter

2 medium onions, chopped

3 ribs celery, chopped

2 cloves garlic, minced

2 cups smoked pulled pork, chopped

2 tablespoons Louisiana hot sauce

1 teaspoon dried sage

1 teaspoon dried thyme

1 tablespoon salt

1 teaspoon finely ground black pepper

2 to 3 cups vegetable broth

Two 8-ounce packages plain cornbread stuffing

I've been making and promoting this recipe for years. It has never caught on, but maybe it will now.

- **Yield: About 10 servings**

Preheat the oven to 350°F.

In a large skillet over medium heat, melt the butter. Add the onion, celery, and garlic and cook until tender.

Add the pork, hot sauce, sage, thyme, salt, and pepper. Stir and cook until the pork is heated through. Add 2 cups of the broth, stir well, and remove from the heat.

Put the stuffing mix in a big bowl. Pour the butter mixture over the stuffing. Toss to mix thoroughly, adding more broth as needed to moisten all the stuffing mix.

Transfer to a 9 × 13-inch baking pan. Cover with foil and place in the oven. Cook for 40 minutes. Remove the foil and cook another 10 minutes. Serve.

Green Bean Smoked Casserole

The Casserole

1 can green beans, drained and sliced lengthwise

1 can or jar small whole onions

2 tablespoons diced pimiento

1 can cream of mushroom soup

¼ cup chopped New Mexican green chiles

The Topping

¼ cup fine breadcrumbs

¼ cup grated Parmesan cheese

2 tablespoons butter, melted

"**D**r. BBQ, do you smoke everything?" Not quite, but I'm trying. Here is the classic Thanksgiving casserole transformed just a little. • **Yield: 4 servings**

Prepare the grill for indirect cooking at 350°F, using apple wood for flavor.

In a lightly buttered 1½-quart casserole, combine the green beans, onions, diced pimiento, mushroom soup, and green chiles. In a bowl, combine the topping ingredients and sprinkle over the top of the casserole.

Place on the grate and smoke, uncovered, for 30 minutes.

Whiskey and Chocolate Pecan Pie

1 cup sugar

¼ cup melted butter

3 eggs, slightly beaten

¾ cup light corn syrup

¼ teaspoon salt

2 tablespoons whiskey

1 teaspoon vanilla extract

½ cup chopped pecans

½ cup chocolate chips

One 9-inch prepared pie shell

This Southern favorite is a great finish for Turkey Day. I love to serve it with chocolate chip ice cream for a double whammy of chocolate. • **Yield: 6 to 8 servings**

Preheat the oven to 375°F.

In a bowl, cream together the sugar and butter. Add the eggs, syrup, salt, whiskey, and vanilla. Mix until blended. Spread pecans and chocolate chips in the bottom of the pie shell. Pour the filling into the shell. Bake for about 45 minutes. Cool before serving.

Drawers, Patio, and Pantry

I call this section of the book Drawers, Patio, and Pantry because I'm going to talk about all the things we keep in those places—the things you need to have around to barbecue, like tools, grills, fuel, and basic rubs and sauces.

The Drawers

Let's start with the drawers. This is where we keep all the knives, spoons, thermometers, and such. Many of us barbecuers have a Rubbermaid container or two in the garage that serve as the drawer, but you get the idea. Here's what I have in mine and why.

Tongs

I have a bunch of short spring tongs that I get at the restaurant supply store. They have different-colored rubber grips. In a restaurant setting, the green ones have a role and the yellow ones have a different role, which helps keep things from cross-contaminating. I'm not usually cooking as many different things as they are, but I like the colors to remind me that I've been using the same pair all day and it's time to get some clean ones. You can also get a nice combination that will match your favorite team's colors. I prefer the short ones made for the kitchen, I just feel that I have a better grip and more dexterity with them. I do

have some longer ones for grilling hot and some real long barbecue tongs for extreme hot grilling and wimpy friends.

Spatulas

I don't seem to use these as much as the tongs. I have a couple of long ones that came with a barbecue set, and I like them and use them. I also have an extra-wide fish spatula that I use for fish and other fragile foods. Last but not least, I have a great big heavy-duty stainless steel custom-made big daddy spatula that Brian Anderson from Grayling, Michigan, made for me. It's badass and you can't buy one anything like it. Brian makes all kinds of things. He even built a big cooker for me one time. If you stop by the Gray Rock Café there in Grayling, maybe he'll build you one, too. I can pick up a whole pork butt or a large brisket with that big spatula. Before I had it, I used a metal pizza getter. That works pretty well, too. I've seen some guys bend the sides up, or trim the shape of the flat part to fit what they wanted to move.

Forks

I never use a fork around the grill. There's just no reason to. It doesn't work very well for picking things up, and it does pierce the meat, which can let some juices get out. Now, I'm not too worried about a quarter teaspoon of juice getting out of a 15-pound brisket, but why keep stabbing at it when a spatula or a couple of pairs of tongs will do the job even better? I do use a fork sometimes to hold a roast that I am carving, and I usually use a fork to put the barbecue in my mouth, but those are the only times.

Brush

I use a typical kitchen brush most of the time. I have a really nice one with a little hook that keeps it from sliding down in the bowl. I got that at a restaurant supply store, too. You really should go to these places. Most of them will sell to you, and they have nicer equipment at lower prices than the fancy kitchen stores. Buy a good brush that looks like the bristles will be staying in place for a long time. I have a big, long barbecue brush, but I can't remember the last time I used it. If the grill and food are too hot to get close to, it's probably not a good time to be putting any sauce on anyway. Those long ones are usually poorly made, so you end up with bristles on your food. My friend Dave DeWitt has an old 1½-inch-wide paintbrush his father passed down to him that has only been used with the grill. It must be at least fifty years old and it *still works fine.*

Pans

This may not be typical barbecue info, but it took me a long time to figure it out, and I wish I'd seen it in a book like this. There are two basic sizes of pan in the restaurant business. One is the hotel pan, and the other is the sheet pan. They are different, but both are universally accepted, and all the racks, steam tables, chafing dishes, lids, and such are interchangeable. There are also cut-down versions that are called ½, ¼, and for hotel pans, even down to ⅙ and ⅑. So, in a restaurant steam table you could have one ½ pan with one item, and two ¼ pans with other items all in one hotel pan–size space. If you pay attention at your next visit to the megabuffet, you'll see many of these sizes in use. The same sizing is used for plastic containers for storage and cold items. The hotel or steam table pan is 12×20 inches and comes in a variety of depths: 2, 4, and 6 inches are the most popular. Sheet pans are 18×26 inches, are typically about an inch deep, and are common in ½ size.

I think you'll find the ½-size sheet pans and the ½-size hotel pans to be very useful in a home kitchen. Look for them at the restaurant supply store, or at the warehouse club. You will also find ½-size and full-size aluminum disposable pans at the warehouse club. I use these all the time around the grill and on it too. They are considerably cheaper than the turkey roaster–type pans you'll see at the grocery store, and made better, too.

Knives

I don't spend a lot of money on knives. I simply can't justify it when I do just fine with my hodgepodge set of knives I've acquired along the way. I do have one fancy German knife that stays sharp very well, but I also have a high-carbon steel knife I got from my grandma that doesn't. I like them both. I find myself mainly using a 10-inch chef's knife and a 6-inch boning knife that came from the restaurant supply store (seeing a pattern here?). They have plastic handles that clean up well. They get sharp and stay sharp plenty long to get the job done, but if somebody grabs one and makes a mistake, they probably won't lose a finger. If one gets dropped, I don't get mad, unless it stabs me in the foot.

I also have a 14-inch Cimetar. This knife looks like something out of a bad Errol Flynn movie with its big curve and pointy tip. When I went to help my buddy Chris Lilly cook at the James Beard House, this was the only kind of knife he had. He told me I'd quickly start to like it and he was right. Chris uses it for everything. I still prefer my other knives for many things, but the Cimetar is a great knife for chopping big piles of pork. It's also good for scaring people.

There is one knife that gets special treatment in my kitchen. That's the carving knife. If you're a barbecue competition cook, slicing the brisket can make or break your week. If that brisket is really tender, your knife had better be up to the challenge or you'll be serving chopped brisket, and that's not a good thing. We all strive for beautiful thin slices.

My longtime choice is an 11-inch slicer made by Cutco. I bought it years ago and have never felt the need for a different knife. It's got some fancy serrated edge that can only be sharpened at the factory, and a skinny blade. The handle isn't that great, but it's not a knife I use much so that doesn't bother me. It stays in a safe place until it's time to slice a roast.

Many of my friends use a 12- or 14-inch slicer with a granton edge. Forschner seems to be a popular brand, and I recently bought one. The granton edge has little oval pockets on the blade. The concept is that the meat won't stick to the blade. It seems to work very well. I also know some good cooks who use an electric knife for carving. I've never used one enough to get good with it, but they seem to work well for some folks.

The last thing I need to touch on here is knife care. This is very important. I take my knives to a sharpening guy at least once a year. Ask a local restaurateur who takes care of his knives, if you can't find a sharpening service in your area. In between sharpening, you'll need to take care of them yourself. A sharpening steel is a must for regular honing. I also have a hand-held sharpener that Bad Byron gave me. Byron is a trained chef and a very successful competition cook. It looks kind of like a pistol grip, with a slot for sharpening the knife and a plastic strap to protect your hand. It works very well. You lean it on the counter and slide the blade along the groove in the slot. One day I was using it improperly and someone asked me a question. When I looked up I sliced my finger. It was a pretty bad cut, so I went to the emergency room, where I got five stitches from a one-armed doctor. I'm not kidding—it was quite an experience. The moral of the story? Don't use your knives or sharpeners improperly.

Cutting Boards

These don't really fit in the drawer but this still seems like the right place to discuss them. I use only plastic or poly cutting boards. I try to buy lightweight ones that are big enough to use but small enough to get into the sink for a hot bath. There are some who claim that wood cutting boards are actually safer, but I just don't buy it. When I get done scrubbing my plastic cutting board in a sink of hot soapy water, it's clean. These also come in colors at the restaurant supply store. In a restaurant setting you would use the green one only for fresh raw veggies and the red one for raw meat only. In the real world you can get one to match your kitchen or your favorite football team.

Thermometers

Taking temperatures is really important. If you can cook at the same grill temp every time and take the meat off when it's just the right temp every time, you will be consistently serving great food off your grill.

First, the thermometer that reads the cooking temp: If your grill or smoker doesn't have one, drill a hole in it and install one. You may need to calibrate this one once in a while. It should have a nut on the back of the dial, so place the tip in boiling water and turn the nut until the needle points to 212°F.

Taking the meat temps is important, too. I get asked all the time for a marinade for chicken that will keep it juicy. The answer is that no marinade will do that if you refuse to take the chicken (or pork or beef or lamb or fish) off the grill when it's done. Without a thermometer, you just can't be sure, so we all just cook it a little longer to be sure. That results in a lot of overdone food that is dry.

The thermometers that have a probe that goes in the meat, with a wire that goes outside the grill to a little readout screen, are very nice and very popular. I don't use these often because I just don't trust them. If I don't put that probe in just the right place in the beginning, I will have a false reading the whole time. I do use the one with the wireless readout that I can take in the house sometimes. That way I can have an idea where things are without even going outside. I always use my handheld thermometer to double-check before taking the meat off the grill.

The reason I like the handheld is because I can take the temp in a few different places and also in a couple different pieces if I'm cooking more than one. I don't like the cheap dial thermometers. They just take too long to get up to temp, and they get out of calibration easily. It's also hard to read that little dial. I do like the $15 digital models; they are slow, too, but at least you can get an accurate reading and you can see the readout.

My all-time favorite is the Thermapen from ThermoWorks. These things are the greatest. Be sure to get the quick-read version. It truly gives you an accurate reading in three to four seconds. It's a little pricey at about $85, but you'll love it.

Here are a few doneness temps.

- Steak medium rare 125°F

- Steak medium 145°F

- Ground beef 155°F

- Pork done safely 137°F

- Pork done just a little pink 145–150°F

- Pork done per the USDA 160°F

- Pork done the way your grandma did it 180°F

- Poultry white meat 160°F

- Poultry dark meat 180°F

The Patio

This is where we talk about the hardware. Grills and smokers, gas, wood, and charcoal. I love them all and they all can be used year-round. Most grills can also serve as a smoker, but the smokers usually don't double as grills. They do well at what I call indirect grilling, though, which is the common ground between the two methods. Many of the recipes in this book call for indirect grilling at 300° to 350°F. Any unit can do this.

I can't possibly tell you how to use every grill because there seem to be hundreds of them. Read the manufacturers' instructions. I know this is hard for most guys, but I did it once and I'm telling you, there was really some good info there. Gas grills are the choice of most barbecuers. My hardcore friends will tell you that true barbecue is only done indirectly, below 275°F, and over wood coals. That's just not true anymore. I go to the Hearth, Patio and Barbecue Association show every year. Those guys are selling thousands of gas grills and calling them barbecues. I'm not going to fight that.

I have a big gas grill that's made by Napoleon. It has three gas burners lined up left to right. I like that configuration because I can light the outside burners and cook indirect. It also has a rotisserie that is also indirect cooking. You just put a little cast-iron box of wood chips over the hot burner and there is smoke. If you begin to really like cooking this way you might consider a smoker, but you can get started on a gas grill. Just make sure you have an extra full propane tank around.

Charcoal grills are the most versatile in my opinion. You can get them hot enough for insanely hot grilling, or use a deflector or just pile the coals on one side and do some real slow smoking. My favorite charcoal grill is always the Big Green Egg, with the insulating and refractory properties that come with the round dome shape and space-age ceramic construction. It's also a world-class smoker. There is nothing that performs better at all the different tasks I ask it to do. The Big Green Egg can grill a steak at 1000°F and smoke a brisket at 225°F without much fussing in between. I've done very well using them in competition.

Smokers come in all different shapes and sizes. The backyard king is the Weber Smokey Mountain. It has all the tradition and craftsmanship that comes from Weber, but it's a real smoker that wins awards at barbecue cookoffs all over the country. It can easily cook in smoker mode at 225°F–350°F, but it isn't really a very convenient direct cooking grill. The configuration of the Weber smoker is common in backyard units. The heat source is on the bottom and a water pan is above the fire to act as a buffer and to add moisture to the cooking chamber. Above that is a series of grills for the meat. In the case of a charcoal cooker, there are vents on top and bottom. There are also gas and electric versions that have no vents, or fixed vents. Cookshack makes a nice little affordable electric backyard model. These all seem to work pretty well and are many different prices. Look around and find one that suits you.

Another popular style of smoker for the backyard is a small inexpensive offset. It's called that because the fire box on the side is dropped down below the cooking chamber in an offset fashion. These units look cool, but the truth is they just don't work very well. They are made to look like their big brothers, but without the ¼-inch steel plate and the other heat-management tools that come with the big offset smokers, it's not a very good way to cook. If you really want to burn down the forest and cook like a big boy, you're gonna need to spend at least a couple thousand dollars.

Last but not least are the pellet cookers. These are almost automatic. They have a switch with either a timer or a thermostat, and they feed in the little wood pellets as needed. I like these very much, especially the Fast Eddy series, also from Cookshack.

Almost all of the recipes in this book can be adapted to whatever you're cooking on. That's why I often use the term "cooker" in the recipes. To me, they are all cookers. You just need to learn how yours works best and make the recipe and the cooker work together.

Gas is gas. Not much to talk about. Charcoal comes in two main types, briquettes and natural lump. The briquettes are a manufactured product, made with molds, while the natural lump is just that, charred lumps of wood. I've used them both extensively. I find that the big national brands are all good. Stay away from rock-bottom cheap stuff. You get what you pay for. There are designer brands of both types out there; if you have access to them they are mostly good products and worth pursuing, but a lot of

money has been won using that K brand of briquette.

Wood is available these days in many different shapes and types. I always use charcoal for heat and wood for flavor. Too much wood can result in oversmoking, and most people don't like that. I use chips more than chunks or logs. I like to spread the smoking stuff all around the charcoal, instead of one big piece in the middle. My favorite wood is always cherry if it's available, and I usually add a little hickory to complement it. My second choice would be pecan. I think these go with everything. Apple is a good substitute. Occasionally I'll use some orange wood. Because I live in Florida, it's kind of a novelty. I don't wander much from these. I just don't see any reason to.

The Pantry

These are the cornerstones of all my barbecue recipes: the rubs, marinades, sauces, and other assorted condiments. I like to put them all in one place in the book so that you can mix and match, or even use them to create your own dish. In most of the recipes where I call for a rub or a sauce, feel free to substitute a different one that looks good to you, or even combine or customize them. I hope that my cookbooks teach you how to cook, instead of just offering up standard recipes.

Barbecue Rubs

Barbecue rubs are simply seasoning blends that I sprinkle on the food. When I make one, I usually start out with salt, sugar, pepper, and usually onion and garlic. From there I use what I'm in the mood for. I don't generally make my rubs very hot. Just add a little cayenne if you want to spice them up.

Year-Round Barbecue Rub

½ cup salt

½ cup **turbinado sugar**

¼ cup **light brown sugar**

2 tablespoons **paprika**

2 tablespoons **lemon pepper**

2 tablespoons **chile powder**

1½ tablespoons **granulated garlic**

1 tablespoon **onion powder**

2 teaspoons **ground cayenne pepper**

½ teaspoon **ground allspice**

½ teaspoon **ground cinnamon**

This is a good basic barbecue rub.

• Yield: About 2 cups

Combine all the ingredients in a bowl and mix well. Store in a tightly capped jar.

Peggy's Favorite Barbecue Rub

¼ cup light brown sugar

2 tablespoons chile powder

1 tablespoon freshly ground black pepper

1 tablespoon salt

1 tablespoon paprika

1 teaspoon dried oregano

1 teaspoon ground cinnamon

1 teaspoon onion powder

1 teaspoon garlic powder

I was one of the first contestants on *All-Star BBQ Showdown,* hosted by Chris Lilly. During my first event, we were discussing who had made the best rub that day. The show is cohosted by the lovely Peggy Bunker, so of course we chose her to be our judge. When the BS finally ended, Peggy had chosen mine as the best, so I named it for her.

• **Yield: About ¾ cup**

Combine all the ingredients in a bowl and mix well. Store in a tightly capped jar.

Big-Time Barbecue Rub

½ cup salt

½ cup turbinado sugar

¼ cup granulated brown sugar

1 tablespoon granulated garlic

1 tablespoon granulated onion

2 tablespoons paprika

2 tablespoons chile powder

2 tablespoons freshly ground black pepper

2 teaspoons ground cayenne pepper

1 tablespoon dried thyme

1 tablespoon ground cumin

1 tablespoon ground nutmeg

This is a very good and basic barbecue rub from my first book, *Dr. BBQ's Big-Time Barbecue Cookbook*. It works well on any food for smoking or grilling

• **Yield:** 1½ **cups**

Combine all the ingredients in a bowl, mix well, and store in an airtight container.

Seasoning Blends

These are a little different than the rubs. They don't always have sugar in them, and they are great for hot grilling, but don't be afraid to try them with low and slow, too.

Groundhog Jerk Seasoning

2 tablespoons onion powder

1 tablespoon ground allspice

1 tablespoon ground thyme

2 teaspoons ground cinnamon

2 teaspoons ground cloves

2 teaspoons brown sugar

2 teaspoons ground dried habanero chile

1 teaspoon freshly ground black pepper

1 teaspoon garlic powder

1 teaspoon ground coriander

½ teaspoon ground nutmeg

½ teaspoon salt

You want a hot one? Here it is. This spicy seasoning was created for smoked groundhog (read "rabbit"), but it works well on other things, too, like chicken and pork.

• Yield: ½ cup

Combine all the ingredients in a bowl, mix well, and store in an airtight container.

Dr. BBQ's Chicken Seasoning

2 tablespoons lemon pepper

2 tablespoons chicken bouillon granules (I like Knorr)

1 tablespoon plus 1 teaspoon granulated garlic

1 tablespoon plus 1 teaspoon dried thyme

2 teaspoons onion powder

2 teaspoons paprika

1 teaspoon salt

½ teaspoon ground cinnamon

½ teaspoon ground cayenne pepper

For some reason, chicken and lemon-based seasonings really go well together. • **Yield: ½ cup**

Combine all the ingredients in a bowl, mix well, and store in an airtight container.

Dr. BBQ's Pork Seasoning

¼ cup turbinado sugar

2 tablespoons ranch dressing dry mix

½ tablespoon coarsely ground black pepper

½ tablespoon salt

½ tablespoon granulated garlic

1 teaspoon dry mustard

1 teaspoon curry powder

1 teaspoon rubbed sage

1 teaspoon celery salt

1 teaspoon paprika

½ teaspoon ground nutmeg

Despite some unusual ingredients, this seasoning works quite well. Trust me. • **Yield: 1 cup**

Combine all the ingredients in a bowl, mix well, and store in an airtight container.

Dr. BBQ's Steak Seasoning

2 tablespoons salt

2 tablespoons turbinado sugar

1½ tablespoons paprika

1 tablespoon coarsely ground black pepper

2 teaspoons granulated garlic

1 teaspoon onion powder

1 teaspoon ground coriander

½ teaspoon ground turmeric

This seasoning can be rubbed on steak immediately before grilling. • **Yield: ½ cup**

Combine all the ingredients in a bowl, mix well, and store in an airtight container.

Dr. BBQ's Five Spice Salt

½ cup salt

2 tablespoons Chinese five spice powder

1 teaspoon granulated garlic

2 teaspoons finely ground black pepper

1 tablespoon granulated brown sugar

Sprinkle this seasoning on pork or lamb chops before grilling. It also works on strongly flavored fish, like fresh tuna steaks. • **Yield: ¾ cup**

Combine all the ingredients in a bowl, mix well, and store in an airtight container.

Dr. BBQ's Creole Seasoning

3 tablespoons salt

1 tablespoon celery salt

3 tablespoons paprika

1 tablespoon granulated garlic

1 tablespoon onion powder

2 teaspoons finely ground black pepper

1 teaspoon ground cayenne pepper

1 tablespoon dried thyme

1 tablespoon dried basil

1 teaspoon dried oregano

Use this on shrimp or sausage that you're going to grill. It also works as a gumbo or jambalaya seasoning. • **Yield: About ¾ cup**

Mix all the ingredients together in a bowl and store in an airtight container.

Barbecue Sauces

Some purists will tell you that real, true barbecue doesn't need sauces (or any seasoning for that matter). Others will tell you that sauces are the most important part of the barbecue. This is similar to the debate over beans in chili con carne, and boils down to personal preference. There are others who will tell you that it's a strictly regional thing. I disagree. I see people use sweet sauce in all the regions and I see people skip the sauce in all the regions. Even the more limited concepts like vinegar sauce or mustard sauce are showing up all over the place. I think that's great. If you like sauces, use them. If you don't like them, skip the following recipes. Some advice from the doctor, though: If you're not sure if the guests want sauce, serve it on the side in little cups. That's always my personal preference. If you sauce the meat yourself, start with just a little sauce since you can always add more. However, if the meat is swimming in sauce, the flavor can be overwhelmed and your great barbecue can't even be tasted.

There are many different kinds of barbecue sauce. I've created some interesting twists for this book.

Dr. BBQ's Peachipotle Barbecue Sauce

1½ cups peach preserves

1 cup ketchup

¼ cup Tabasco chipotle sauce

¼ cup honey

1 tablespoon cider vinegar

½ teaspoon rubbed sage

This is a combination I've been meaning to try for a while now. I wish I'd gotten around to it sooner because it's a good one. • **Yield: 3 cups**

Combine all the ingredients in a saucepan. Heat to a simmer, mixing, just until blended.

Dr. BBQ's Race Day Barbecue Sauce

2 cups ketchup

2 tablespoons chile powder

2 tablespoons dry mustard

1 tablespoon Worcestershire sauce

1 tablespoon soy sauce

1 tablespoon garlic powder

1 tablespoon onion powder

2 tablespoons molasses

¼ cup Tabasco, or some other vinegar-based hot sauce

I invented this while watching the Daytona 500 (page 69).
• Yield: 2½ cups

Combine all the ingredients in a saucepan. Whisk together while bringing just to a simmer.

Remove from heat and serve, or cool for later.

Blender Barbecue Sauce

1 medium red onion, chopped

3 jalapeños, seeded, deveined, and chopped

3 cloves garlic, pressed

One 14.5-ounce can diced tomatoes

1 cup apple juice

½ cup honey

2 tablespoons Worcestershire sauce

2 tablespoons cider vinegar

1 tablespoon salt

1 tablespoon freshly squeezed lime juice

2 teaspoons freshly ground black pepper

2 teaspoons dried thyme

½ teaspoon ground nutmeg

½ teaspoon liquid smoke

I started out to make a chunky barbecue sauce, but I don't like chunky barbecue sauces, so this one ended up in the blender. Then I liked it. • **Yield: 4 cups**

In a saucepan, sauté the onion, jalapeños, and garlic in a little oil until soft. Add all the other ingredients, bring to a simmer, and cook 15 minutes.

Put in a blender and puree.

Green Chile Barbecue Sauce

3 cups Blender Barbecue Sauce (above)

1 cup New Mexican green chiles, roasted, peeled, and chopped

New Mexican green chiles seem to be everywhere these days. • **Yield: 4 cups**

Combine the barbecue sauce and the green chiles in a bowl and mix well.

Condiments

There are 56,213 different brands of condiments at the supermarket. Okay, I made that up but there sure are a bunch of them, so why am I giving some recipes here? Because mine are more original and better-tasting than the store-bought ones. Feel free to experiment with these, too. There are no set rules.

Dr. BBQ's Hot Dog Sauce

1 pound twice-ground chuck

1 large onion, chopped fine

2 cloves garlic, minced

One 6-ounce can tomato paste

1 cup water

1 tablespoon sugar

1 tablespoon prepared yellow mustard

1 tablespoon dried minced onion

2 teaspoons chile powder

1 teaspoon Worcestershire sauce

1 teaspoon salt

½ teaspoon celery seed

½ teaspoon ground cumin

½ teaspoon coarsely ground black pepper

It's good on burgers, too, and even noodles.
• Yield: 12 or more servings

Brown the ground beef in a skillet, adding the onion halfway through. Add the minced garlic when meat is nearly done. Add the remaining ingredients; stir well to combine.

Simmer over low heat 15 minutes, uncovered.

Dave's Homemade Honey Mustard

⅔ cup white mustard seeds

1 tablespoon dry mustard powder

1 cup water

2 tablespoons whole wheat flour

½ cup white wine vinegar

¼ cup honey

We're so used to buying commercial mustards that we forget that it's pretty easy to make your own. This is a salt-free, fairly sweet mustard that's great on just about everything. • **Yield: About 1 cup**

Note: This recipe requires advance preparation.

Blend the mustard seeds and powder in a spice grinder, leaving the mixture slightly grainy. Transfer to a bowl and then mix in the water, stirring to blend. Cover the bowl and let sit for 24 hours, stirring occasionally.

Stir the flour into the mustard base. Then add the vinegar and honey and stir well. This mustard will keep for months in the refrigerator.

Hot Horseradish Mustard

½ cup dry mustard

¼ cup yellow mustard seeds

⅓ cup cider vinegar

2 tablespoons prepared horseradish, drained

2 teaspoons habanero hot sauce

1 clove garlic, minced

3 tablespoons honey

1 teaspoon brown sugar

½ cup white wine vinegar

¼ teaspoon ground white pepper

Yield: About 2 cups

Note: This one requires some serious advance preparation.

To make the mustard, combine the dry mustard, mustard seeds, and the cider vinegar in a bowl and stir to mix. Allow the mixture to sit for 15 minutes.

Place 1 tablespoon of the horseradish, the hot sauce, and the garlic in a blender or food processor and puree until smooth, adding a little water if necessary. Strain the mixture into the mustards.

Combine the mustard mixture, honey, brown sugar, and pepper along with ½ cup hot water in a saucepan and bring to a simmer over a low heat; stirring constantly, until slightly thickened. Remember, the mustard will thicken as it cools, so don't cook it too long. Cool the mustard, add the remaining horseradish, and add the white wine vinegar to thin. Spoon the mustard into a sterilized jar and refrigerate for 1 week before using.

Salsas

As with commercial barbecue sauces, there's a ton of salsa out there but the best ones are homemade.

Que-ribbean Salsa

1½ cups finely diced pineapple

3 tomatillos, husks removed, finely diced

½ habanero chile, stem and seeds removed, finely diced, or substitute ground habanero

2 tablespoons chopped fresh cilantro

1 teaspoon grated ginger

2 tablespoons barbecue sauce

Here is a salsa without tomatoes, believe it or not.
• Yield: 2 cups

In a bowl, combine the pineapple, tomatillos, chile, cilantro, and ginger and toss them with the barbecue sauce.

Dr. BBQ's Grilled Southwestern Salsa

6 green New Mexican chiles (Anaheim chiles will work as a substitute)

4 jalapeños

2 large tomatoes

4 tomatillos

2 medium onions, quartered

¼ cup chopped fresh cilantro

3 cloves garlic, crushed

This is an all-purpose salsa that can be served with tortilla chips, enchiladas, tacos, and as an accompaniment to grilled entrées, as well as used as an ingredient in recipes. • **Yield: 1½ cups**

Prepare the grill for direct grilling at high heat. Place the chiles, jalapeños, tomatoes, tomatillos, and onions on a grill. Grill the vegetables until the skins burn and pop, turning occasionally.

Peel the vegetables, removing the stems and seeds from the chiles, and chop coarsely. Transfer to a bowl, add the cilantro and garlic, mix well, and serve.

Marinades

Marinades are great for flavoring the food before cooking, and they can be very creative. They also provide moisture, but they penetrate the meat slowly, which is why many cuts of meat are marinated overnight. I often inject the marinade to get the flavor down deep inside, but that won't work with any marinade that has things in it that will clog the needle.

Po'Boy Italian Dressing Marinade

½ cup olive oil

¼ cup canola oil

¼ cup balsamic vinegar

½ teaspoon salt

½ teaspoon finely ground black pepper

½ teaspoon dried thyme

½ teaspoon dried oregano

½ teaspoon dried red pepper flakes

This recipe has many lives. It will work well with a pasta salad, or to marinate a pork tenderloin. But it really shines in the po'boy sandwich from Bad Byron (page 99). • **Yield: 1 cup**

Put all the ingredients in a blender and puree for 15 seconds.

Dr. BBQ's Soy Sauce Marinade

¼ cup Kikkoman soy sauce

1 tablespoon rice wine vinegar

1 tablespoon oyster sauce

½ teaspoon white pepper

¼ teaspoon granulated garlic

¼ teaspoon ground allspice

Here's my favorite Asian-inspired marinade that goes well with anything. It's a little salty and full of flavor. • **Yield: ½ cup**

In a small bowl, whisk all the ingredients together.

Ray's Whiskey Marinade

¼ cup Tennessee whiskey

2 tablespoons honey

1 tablespoon Worcestershire sauce

1 tablespoon Kikkoman soy sauce

1 tablespoon balsamic vinegar

1 tablespoon Tabasco sauce

1 teaspoon granulated garlic

1 teaspoon red chile powder

It's risky to give whiskey to a barbecue guy, but I'll chance it here. • **Yield: ¾ cup**

In a small bowl, mix all the ingredients together.

Lemon Garlic Marinade

8 cloves garlic

½ cup lemon juice

½ cup white wine

½ teaspoon ground
cayenne pepper

This marinade is excellent for chicken and turkey.
• Yield: 1 cup

In a food processor, puree the garlic and then add the lemon juice,
white wine, and cayenne.

Anything But

This is the common barbecue miscellaneous category, also known as the stuff that doesn't fit anywhere else.

Tzatziki Sauce

1 cup grated cucumber, drained

2 cups plain yogurt

Juice of ½ lemon

Salt and freshly ground black pepper to taste

Here is the classic gyro sauce, but it can be a salad dressing, too. • **Yield: 3 cups**

Try to squeeze as much water as possible out of the cucumber. In a bowl, mix the yogurt, lemon juice, and the cucumber. Check for salt and pepper and add as needed.

Refrigerate for at least 2 hours.

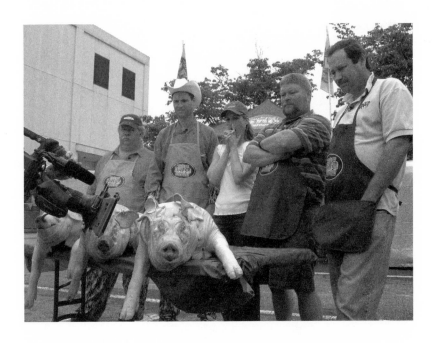

Grilled Onion Guacamole

2 tablespoons corn oil

2 tablespoons fresh lemon juice

1 tablespoon red wine vinegar

1 teaspoon crushed black pepper

½ teaspoon ground cumin

¾ teaspoon salt

1 large red onion, sliced ¼ inch thick

3 ripe avocados, peeled, pitted, and diced

3 serrano chiles, stems removed, seeded, and chopped

1 large tomato, diced

2 cloves garlic, minced

1 small bunch cilantro, chopped

2 teaspoons freshly squeezed lime juice

This is a great grilled twist to guacamole. Try it on your burgers. • **Yield: 6 servings**

Combine the oil, lemon juice, vinegar, black pepper, cumin, and salt in a bowl and mix well. Add the onion slices and marinate for 1 hour. Drain off the marinade and grill the onion slices on a hot grill for 3 minutes per side. In a bowl, mix the slices with the remaining guacamole ingredients, cover, and keep at room temperature until ready for use.

Poblano Vinaigrette

6 poblano chiles, roasted, peeled, stems and seeds removed

½ cup white wine vinegar

¼ cup vegetable oil

2 tablespoons chopped fresh cilantro

4 cloves garlic

2 shallots

2 teaspoons Dijon mustard

Juice of 2 limes

Kosher salt and freshly ground black pepper to taste

This can be used as a marinade or a salad dressing.
• **Yield: 2½ cups**

To make the vinaigrette, place all the ingredients in a blender and process until smooth.

Scottie's Creole Butter

1 pound butter

1 can beer of choice

1 tablespoon Big-Time BBQ
Rub (page 279)

1 tablespoon paprika

1 tablespoon freshly
ground white pepper

1 tablespoon sea salt

1 tablespoon garlic powder

1 tablespoon onion powder

1 tablespoon dry mustard

1 tablespoon freshly and
finely ground black pepper

1 teaspoon ground
cayenne pepper

This recipe was inspired by my friend Scottie Johnson from Chicago. It appeared in my first book, but it had to be here, too, so I could make "The Ultimate Turkey" for my Thanksgiving menu (page 264). • **Yield: About 2½ cups**

Melt the butter in saucepan and add the beer and spices. Mix well. Let cool, then inject.

Dr. BBQ's Pork Mop

1 cup apple juice

1 cup beer

½ cup cider vinegar

1 stick butter, melted

2 tablespoons whiskey

1 tablespoon
Worcestershire sauce

A mop or sop is basically a marinade or basting liquid that is applied during the actual cooking process. • **Yield: About 3 cups**

Combine all the ingredients and puree in a blender.

Lemon Mop

1 cup olive oil

Juice of 2 lemons

2 cloves garlic, crushed

1 teaspoon dried oregano

This is great on chicken but can be used on shrimp as well. • **Yield: 1½ cups**

To make the mop, whisk all the ingredients together in a bowl.

Orange-Honey Glaze

1 cup orange juice, freshly squeezed preferred

¼ cup honey

1 teaspoon garlic powder

1 teaspoon dried oregano

This one goes well on pork or ham cooked indirectly. • **Yield: 1¼ cups**

Place all the ingredients for the glaze in a blender or food processor and puree until smooth.

References

Anon. "Cinco de Mayo." Web-Holidays.com, http://web-holidays.com, December 2004.

Anon. "Lucky Food Around the World." AllRecipes.com, http://allrecipes.com, December 2004.

Anon. "New Year's Customs Around the World." Web-Holidays.com, http://web-holidays.com, December 2004.

Anon. "Summer Solstice Celebrations: Ancient and Modern." ReligiousTolerance.org, http://www.religioustolerance.org, January 2005.

Anon. *Sunset Barbecue Cook Book*. Menlo Park, CA: Lane Publishing Co., 1951.

Anon. "The Winter Solstice." Equinox and Solstice.com, http://www.equinox-and-solstice.com, December 2004.

Anon. "Valentine's Day." Web-Holidays.com, http://web-holidays.com, December 2004.

Beard, James. *Barbecue with Beard*. New York: Golden Press, 1975.

Everett, Linda. *Retro Barbecue: Tasty Recipes for the Grillin' Guy*. Portland, OR: Collector's Press, 2002.

Fox, Selena. "Saturnalia." Circle Sanctuary. www.circlesanctuary.com, December 2004.

Haggerty, Bridget. "Corned Beef and Cabbage—The Feeding of a Myth." Irish Customs and Cultures, http://www.irishcultureandcustoms.com/2Kitch/aCBeefCabge.html, December 2004.

Maguire, Tara. "Use Creativity for Super Bowl Get-Together." Lubbock Online, http://lubbockonline.com, December 2004.

Staten, Vince. *Jack Daniel's Old Time Barbecue Cookbook*. Louisville, KY: The Sulgrave Press, 1991.

Wedeck, H. E. *Dictionary of Aphrodisiacs*. London: Bracken Books, 1994.

Index